TEN TIPS
FOR PRODUCING A TOP QUALITATIVE RESEARCH STUDY

BY

STACEY EDMONSON
SAM HOUSTON STATE UNIVERSITY

BEVERLY IRBY
SAM HOUSTON STATE UNIVERSITY

PEARSON

BOSTON   NEW YORK   SAN FRANCISCO
MEXICO CITY   MONTREAL   TORONTO   LONDON   MADRID   MUNICH   PARIS
HONG KONG   SINGAPORE   TOKYO   CAPE TOWN   SYDNEY

ISBN-13: 978-0-205-52433-4
ISBN-10:   0-205-52433-8

Printed in the United States of America

10 9 8 7 6 5 4 3 2 1   11 10 09 08 07

Table of Contents

INTRODUCTION

TEN TIPS FOR PRODUCING A TOP QUALITATIVE RESEARCH STUDY

You are probably in your doctoral studies program and are in a qualitative methods course. Already, you have received your syllabus, and your professor indicates that this semester you will learn while doing—by completing a qualitative study and preparing a paper that has potential for publication. Overwhelmed? Yes—is an understatement. You need to determine a topic, conduct a literature review, complete an Internal Review Board Human Subjects application, research the topic, and write the paper. How do you get everything done in a semester and still produce a top quality piece of research that may be publishable? This workbook does not deal with a mixed method research design; rather, it is strictly related to qualitative research only. Additionally, this workbook does not intend to substitute for your textbook that will provide theoretical and background information needed to understand qualitative research.

This workbook is designed to help you through the process of research and the writing of the paper. By learning the 10 tips to a top quality qualitative manuscript, you can submit a final product that is reflective of your best work and which reflects the best on your university and program should you and your professor decide it is worthy of submission for publication review. With this workbook, you can work quickly through the process of the development, data gathering, and writing of a qualitative study in one semester. If you are in control of these 10 tips, you can actually apply these to the dissertation process as well.

Tip #1: Select Your Topic

How do you select your topic? In selecting the topic, you must consider the method as well? Sometimes the topic or focus of the study will require a specific type of method. For the purpose of the semester-long research project, you must keep that pointer in mind. For example, an ethnographic case study on a particular cultural aspect of an ethnic group may take spending time within the culture—from one month to one year or more. For the dissertation, that may work, but for the semester course product, it will not. Chapter 1 will give you specific principles on how you can select an appropriate topic for your semester assignment.

Tip #2: Determine Your Purpose

Your purpose is critical. Of course in a qualitative study, we know that sometimes, the topic is known, but the purpose may be fuzzy initially. We are going to work toward a clearly defined purpose for the semester project. Without such, the project will not be completed. Therefore, it is very important for you to first determine what it is you wish to do surrounding your topic. Chapter 2 will provide information on and examples of clearly defined purposes, Tip #2, for the completion of a project within a semester.

Tip #3: Develop your Introduction, Review of Literature, and Problem

It is assumed that you have been reading the professional literature or that you have been attending seminars and conferences in which research has been presented. We are certain that you have been attending sessions that have stirred your interest. Therefore, you know something about your topic and what the underlying problems might be. You will need to get into the literature and be certain that whatever it is that has interested you has not already interested someone else many times over and that the issue has been researched in-depth both quantitatively and qualitatively with the same population or documents in which you have an targeted. Tip #3, how to develop your introduction, review of literature, and problem for qualitative research, is presented in Chapter 3.

Tip #4: Determine Your Theoretical Framework

The Theoretical Framework is important to your study, and it is specifically related to the purpose, problem, and significance. A Theoretical Framework can be a formal, specific theory, several theories, or a collection of studies related to the concept you are studying. How to find your Theoretical Framework, Tip #4, and determine how it will interweave throughout your study will be reviewed in Chapter 4.

Tip #5: Go through the Internal Review Board (IRB) and Develop your Research Design

We know that you are probably a bit nervous when you are asked by your professor, "So, Ms. Garza, what do you think your research design might be and tell us why?" There you are—on the spot. The activities we include will assist you in being prepared to provide a sound response to your professor, but most importantly for yourself as you develop your research design. Several typical research designs will be reviewed in Chapter 5 for Tip #5 is presented along with samples of Human Subjects Forms for submission to a university's internal review board.

Tip #6: Develop your Context, Sample, and Instrument

Sharing with your readers the context and sample are important to the in-depth understanding of your study. You will need to take your readers to the place(s) in which your study takes place. You will need to describe how you decided on your sample by going into detail about: (a) who, (b) what, (c) where, (d) when, and (e) how. Tip #6, Chapter 6, will guide you to building a better component of your study—the context and sample.

Tip #7: Increase the Reliability and Validity of your Study

You will need to begin to consider how your entire study will be a valid and reliable study, something of extreme importance in qualitative work just as applicability and generalizability are of utmost import to quantitative studies. We will review for you and provide examples of ways in which you may improve the validity and reliability of the study in Chapter 7.

Tip #8: Collect Data

For Tip #8 in Chapter 8, we will review varying types of data that you may collect depending on the type of research design you will be using in your study. Additionally, we will discuss ways to collect the data with differing types of common techniques and data sources. Instrumentation, or your tool for collecting data, is as important in a qualitative study as in a quantitative study.

Tip #9: Analyze Data

Steps in analyzing various types of data will be presented in Chapter 9. Analysis and interpretation of the data is the stage of the study that can make or break the study. Why? The answer is simple. If you have devised a beautiful plan and gathered the data and you cannot adequately analyze and interpret data, then the study is of not worth. Therefore, we want to assist you in determining well what your findings actually are. Sample transcripts for practice coding are provided as well.

Tip #10: Write the Paper, Revise, & Edit

By this point, you will have written components of the paper. In fact, in Chapter 10, we will provide you with a timeline for completing a qualitative study within a semester-long course. All components of the paper that have not been reviewed in Tips 1–9, will be reviewed in this chapter. Common errors in writing, using a particular style manual, will also be noted for your convenience.

It is our hope that this workbook will assist in relieving your stress by taking you by the hand and guiding you through the development of a qualitative research study and subsequent paper in a simple step by step format.

TIP #1 SELECT YOUR TOPIC

It is the first day of your first qualitative research class, and your professor says, "Now let's look at the syllabus. The major performance event for this class will be the actual design, implementation, and completion of a qualitative research project." At first thought you think, "Okay, that doesn't sound so bad." But, the next statement out of your professor's mouth delivers the blow—your professor continues with a smile, "And this project will be developed into a research paper with potential for publication by the end of the semester."

You freeze—an overwhelming feeling takes over, because, in addition to completing a research paper that has the potential for publication, you have to read the required text and several required articles, complete critiques, and get through as much literature on own your topic as you can! But wait- hold the fort, there is good news, because we know—

You can do this! Select your topic and organize your time.

You can do it!

But—the only way to get this "what seems to be an insurmountable task" done and to do a quality job is to begin. So here we go! Let's begin.

You will begin by selecting a topic—this topic may or may not lead to your life's work or even your dissertation, but all of these exercises will help you to learn the process of "doing" qualitative research. Yes, you will need to read additional textbooks on and examples of qualitative research to become as familiar with the procedures as possible, but for now, we will simply begin chipping away, task by task, so that you can complete your paper this semester.

A REFLECTION ON THE BEGINNING

Even when I worked with second grade gifted students on qualitative research, I began with a simple series of questions to them. They went something like this, "Generate as many ideas on your paper as you can related to your interests. Now, what interests you most? Mark about three."

If I had some second graders who were having difficulty, I would say, "Well, let's see. Have you ever wondered about something like why the grass is green, why the sky is blue, how an airplane flies, or why sound comes and goes as a car zooms by and what that might be and relate to in our natural world?"

Inevitably, the children would generate many ideas related to their interests. We would duly note those, and afterward we would embark on a fieldtrip to the county library and school library since these times were prior to the days of the Internet. There in the library, the students would begin their quest and discover as much as they could before they initiated their writing and made their final decisions on their topics.

I can recall many of the studies, but one stands out about a once thriving community of Graysport, Mississippi, that now lies at the bottom of a flood control lake, Grenada Lake established in 1954.

Figure 1.1 *Ariel photo of Grenada Lake*
Used with permission, Grenada Lake Field Office, Grenada, MS.

The child was able to find historical documents, interview some elderly people who once lived in the community, and take photos of artifacts under the water when the water was drained from the northern end of the lake for a period of time. The report was a fascinating piece of qualitative work for a seven-year-old. I tell you this about working with gifted children, because you too, as gifted individual adults, can complete a fascinating study in a short amount of time; so now let's begin. Basically, there are three steps in selecting a topic.

Step 1: Move Toward Interest

The first step is to do just as the second graders with whom I worked did. Consider as many alternative areas of interest as possible.

Take a piece of paper; write those ideas, and then order them (Figure 1.2). If you just absolutely cannot think of a topic, you may speak to one of your professors. Usually, professors are conducting research, so they may have a topic ready for you to investigate. Of course, since you began your graduate program, you may have been focusing on one topic.

If so, then the selection and completion of the problem will be much easier since you have your topic of interest, and since you have reviewed the literature.

We must provide you with a note of caution related to your selected topic and your knowledge of the subject. This cautionary note is based on an incident related to a dissertation proposal, but the essence of the concern is the same as it revolves around the selection of the dissertation topic in terms of interest and knowledge of the topic.

My Interests
1. Bilingual (but I really don't know much about it)
2. principal behavior
3. climate in schools
4. counselors as leaders
5. principal leadership and impact on students

Figure 1.2. *Interest chart.*

Recently we had a student, who had worked hard for two years on a topic of interest for her dissertation. She even had a portion of her review of the literature complete, but upon close examination, we determined the student really did not have the background to handle a dissertation on the topic. This was no fault of the student; rather, the courses in which the student had to write about the topic were never as scrutinizing of the topic as was the proposal class which is the final hoop students must jump through in order to get to the proposal stage with their dissertation advisory committee. The student and the professor actually discovered together that quite a bit of depth related to the literature was missing from the preliminary proposal.

Have an interest in your topic, but also have some background in your topic.

We found the student was interested in the topic due to some personal family issues, but the student (a) had never taught in the field she planned to study, (b) had no in-depth understanding of the field, (c) had not attended conferences on the topic, and (d) had not read and comprehended the latest research on the topic. In fact, it was difficult for the student to discuss the breadth of the literature since she did not have a clear operational understanding of the issues.

9

Therefore, our note of caution is to not only have an interest the topic, but also, to have some level of expertise or experience in the area as well. That being said—there are several places to look for topics to study. You may find a topic of interest from reading the latest journals in your field. Scholars of published research studies usually will suggest additional areas to research.

For example, in this excerpt from one of my articles that was published in the *Advancing Women in Leadership Journal*, we made a recommendation for further research.

> A final question for further thought is that if general research findings are antithetical to the practice of inclusion without structured support for women, how well are the women in such organizations fairing in comparison to their male counterparts in terms of stress management, job satisfaction, skill development, mentoring, networking, and career advancement. (Irby & Brown, 1998, ¶29)

As you read recent dissertations from your university and other universities, you will find hundreds of recommendations for further research. Following are two such examples.

> *Example 1.* Another possible area to consider in future research should be the effects of bullying on overall student performance… Intervention strategies and bully prevention programs need to be studied over time to determine how successful they are in decreasing or altogether eliminating bullying and other forms of school violence…. (Dornfield-Januzzi, 2006, p. 82)

> *Example 2.* Future research should continue to examine the clients' views of counseling. Additional perspectives should also be examined; counselor and family perceptions of self-injury would add to the research and, I believe will provide clinicians with a broader understanding of this phenomenon. (Foster, 2006, p. 316-317)

In addition to reading, you may attend a conference presentation, such as at the American Educational Research Association or the American Counseling Association, on a research topic of interest. Usually at these meetings the researchers and scholars suggest research that is warranted based on their own work.

Keep your eyes and ears open for good topics to research.

Once you have a topic, you may want to meet with the reference librarian at your university's library. Most university libraries have special services for masters and doctoral students which consist of such things as giving them tips on places to search (that the student might not be aware of) to doing searches for the students when the students have not been able to find something they should have. Such services may vary from student to student.

Jess Nevins, a reference librarian at Sam Houston State University, indicated, in an online chat via the university's library reference desk site, the following, "What we do varies from student to student, depending on what the students need and how much help they need." He said, "I had one student looking for material on the management styles of administrators in Turkish universities. For my own research I'd been doing some work in the catalog of the Turkish National Library catalog, so I showed her that site and gave her some tips on how best to use it. That was all she needed. On the other hand, I've had some students who've needed more help, and I had to run some searches for them when they just couldn't figure out how to do the search themselves" (personal communication, October 15, 2006). You may not be aware of all the services that you library offers in the way of assisting you with selecting a topic and in the way of saving you fruitless hours of work.

Step 2: **Consider Your Topic**

There are three considerations related to the selection of your topic. You will want to consider the amount of published research on your topic, the level of controversy that surrounds your topic, and the global nature of your topic.

Consideration Related to Amount of Published Research

Upon first glance, a topic that perhaps you have found little about in the research literature may appear to be a negative thing. We hear many students say, "But there is just nothing in the literature!"

Now, let's look at how that could be a positive situation. First, you will need to address the topic from a related literature approach. Second, you have a problem with your study that you have already addressed—that is—a paucity of literature on the topic you have selected. Your work can add to the literature base, and that would be positive.

Consideration of Controversial Topics

Most of qualitative research has as its center the discovery of human experience or perspective. Historical contexts of qualitative research focus on social connections, movements, and change. It is concerned with political implications and guided by sensitivity to "others" who are being studied. Given this logic, qualitative research will always likely be situated in controversy. Now, this is not bad. Controversy surrounding your topic can be interesting both to you and your readers, and it may have great implications for those who find themselves impacted by your study.

Consideration of Your Topic Globally

Your topic likely is being studied in another part of the country or around the world in a differing context. Once I heard at a conference I attended on creativity with Paul Torrance that at any given time around the world at least seven ideas of a similar nature are being generated. It would be good to have your reference librarian assist you in checking other publications around the world for your topic. You might connect with the person who has or is completing research in a different context. Find out what emerged from that person's research.

Step 3: Narrow Your Topic and Plan Your Time

Once you have a general topic, you will need to narrow your topic, particularly to complete it within the timeframe of a one-semester course.

Narrow Your Topic

We have often seen doctoral students with noble ambitions. They want to solve all problems in a semester study, thesis, or dissertation. You first must come to reality and understand that for the purposes of the semester course in qualitative research, a narrowed, focused topic is necessary so that you will not begin with an overwhelmed frustrated feeling. You have already brainstormed your list of topics, checked those topics in the published research studies related to the topics, and you settled on the top three.

Keep your topic narrow enough to be significant, but doable.

Now simply do a webbing activity that will help you narrow the topic and that will lead you to the next step of developing your purpose. Figure 1.3 depicts a webbed topic as we narrow the topic for study. Depicted is a beginning web. Perhaps we select the parent involvement component. At that point, we would need to conduct another webbing activity so that we can then narrow that topic again.

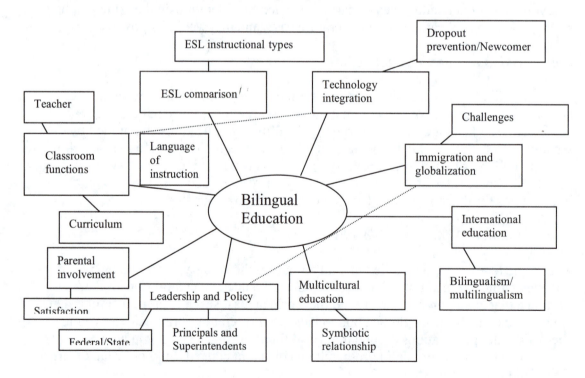

Figure 1.3. *Webbing activity for topic.*

Plan Your Time

The first thing you need to do is to look at your syllabus. Ask these questions: When are the sections due? When is the final paper due? Now, based on the answers to those questions, make a backward map of time.

Be certain you allow time for someone else to edit your paper. On many university campuses there is a writing center that assists students in editing their papers. Check that out as it is usually a part of your fee structure that you have paid. You know your needs in terms of writing. You know if you will need extra time to conduct your research in the library or online. You know if you are a fast, medium, or slow-paced thinker and, thus, writer. It takes some people longer to plan their thoughts and get them on paper than others. Always be certain to plan for glitches in time. Always make plans for more time instead of less. Figure 1.4 provides you with a backward map of time.

Due Date: _____

Begin Date: _____

Weekly deadlines:

Research Paper Part	Week Due
_____	_____
_____	_____
_____	_____

Figure 1.4. *Backward map of deadlines*

Concluding Thoughts

A good topic is worth 1000 minutes. With a good topic that is narrow enough, you can actually conduct a sound study within a four-month time frame. Remember, you can do this! Believe that you can and have no fear. The remainder of this manual will assist you completing your task.

Remember this, qualitative research can be a lot of fun! It really gets to the why and how of people's lived experiences, the why and how of phenomena, or the why and how of societal dilemmas.

There will be many new terms you will learn during your course—terms you have not heard before in a quantitative research program of study, but these are terms that will aid you in conceptualizing the process of qualitative research. So, as you choose your topic, consider what you already know about qualitative research and how this topic will fit into the premises of such research.

Target Activities

Target 1.   Select the Topic and Develop Your Timeline

A. To stay on target, you will need to select your topic. In order to do so, develop and interest chart; then use a web activity to think about various aspects of a topic or topics to narrow your final selection.

B. Develop a timeline in order to complete your study within the semester. Use the outline provided of the backward map.

Due Date: _____

Begin Date: _____

Weekly deadlines:

Research Paper Part	Week Due
_____	_____
_____	_____
_____	_____
_____	_____
_____	_____
_____	_____
_____	_____
_____	_____
_____	_____

References

Dornfield-Januzzi, J. (2006). *Adult perceptions of bullying by boys and girls in middle school.* Fordham University. DAI-A 67/03.

Foster, V. (2006). *A qualitative investigation of the counseling experiences of college-aged women with a history of self.* The College of William and Mary. DAI-A 67/03.

Irby, B. J., & Brown, G. (1998). Exploratory study regarding the status of women's educational administrative support organizations. *Advancing Women in Leadership Journal.* Retrieved on September 15, 2006 from http://www.advancingwomen.com/awl/winter98/awlv2_irby6final.html.

TIP #2 DETERMINE YOUR PURPOSE

Now that you have selected your topic and narrowed it, it is time to determine where you will be headed during the semester. Your purpose statement provides the map to get to your intended destination. We note that there are two views of qualitative research—it can lean toward a structured approach or toward an unstructured, inductive approach. Bogdan and Biklen (2007) discussed and explained these two possibilties within qualitative research, and they indicated "...the design process involves negotiation between you and the informants over what the study will be. You enter the field with an idea, but you must negotiate its pertinence, worth, and value with the people you will study" (p. 55). In this manual, we work from a slightly more structured approach so that you can accomplish your task within one semester. It is from this perspective that we now enter into assisting you with developing a purpose for your research—again, the purpose is the road map that gets you to where you are going.

> *We present a slightly more structured approach to qualitative research, so that you can accomplish your task in a semester.*

Step 1: Know What a Purpose Includes

A purpose statement, fairly easy to construct in your mind, may be more difficult to get exact on paper. It is a bit more difficult to clarify on paper, because, in your mind, you know exactly what you intend to do, but readers may not understand unless the purpose is clearly written.

> *The purpose statement will guide you on your journey and will serve as an advanced organizer for your readers.*

Not only will the purpose guide you on your journey, but also it will assist others in knowing where you are headed and will act as an advance organizer for your readers. If it is not clear, then confusion is created for the readers.

You have already read and listed subtopics in the webbing activity you did as you selected your topic. Look at the branches of the web on your subtopic. What are the most interesting subtopics you generated?

What is one of those areas you want to study, or could a couple of those be combined? Think about those carefully and look briefly through your notes from the literature you reviewed for your general topic to see if such topics have been reviewed in the past.

We will provide an example for you. Here, we use a bilingual parent involvement web, and we will look at various branches that we could develop. Look at Figure 2.1.

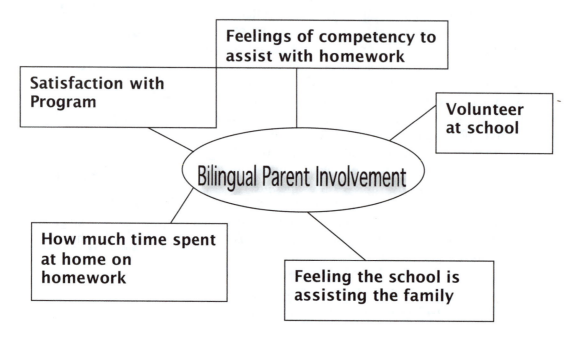

Figure 2.1. *Webbed activity of a subtopic of interest*

Let's consider the webbed activity. First, you would like to know something about parents of bilingual children and their satisfaction with a new preschool curriculum program.

How would you begin a purpose statement? There are three simple rules of thumb. Remember to state exactly what it is you will do. Now, in this case, since you are not proposing as in a dissertation proposal, you will want to write the purpose in past tense as if you have (and you will have) completed the study.

There are three major components of that purpose statement: topic, measured components, and clarity. Measured components in qualitative research means that the components that you are initially interested in investigating are named.

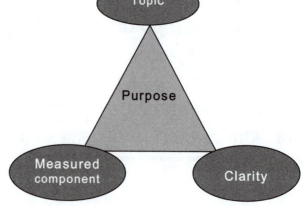

Generally, your purpose statement will be able to be written in one sentence. The purpose (written in past tense for since the study will have been completed at publication) that we might craft from the aforementioned interest in parent involvement and bilingual education could be stated: "The purpose of my study was to determine how parents of bilingual children perceive the effectiveness of the preschool integrated curriculum which has been used in six months related to their children's literacy development."

Examine the purpose statement. Is the topic named? Yes. The topic is noted as—how parents of bilingual children perceive a specific intervention related to their children's literacy development. Is there one or more measured components? Yes. Measured components are: to determine how parents perceive….curriculum…on literacy development. Is it clear where you are guiding the reader? Yes. Would your reader know where you were headed as he/she reads the study? Yes. The reader would expect to see results in those component areas. Now, if you were to answer "no" to any of those questions, then you would need to clarify your purpose.

An example of a purpose related to this that would need clarifying follows: "The purpose of my study was to investigate parents of bilingual children who have been involved in an intervention." First, we have a topic—it is something to do with parents of bilingual children. Second, we do not have measured components, and third, clarity is lacking. We do not know if it is the "parents" who have been involved in an intervention or the "children," and what type of intervention it is. So, clarity is needed.

Step 2:   **Write Clear Purpose Statements**

Before you begin writing purpose statements, you may want to think with sticky notes about the parts of the purpose statement. For example, you can take sticky notes and write the topic and all the components you are interested in studying. See Figure 2.2 for an example of the aforementioned statement. Once you have all your ideas written on your sticky notes, put the ideas together in a logical manner to write your purpose.

Figure 2.3. *Use sticky notes to brainstorm your purpose.*

Following are several other purpose statements. A discussion on the revisions for clarity follows each example.

> *Example 1.* "The purpose of my study was to investigate how homeless shelters are seen by mothers." Let's examine this statement for topic, measured components, and clarity. First, you can see a topic about homeless shelters and mothers. However, it is unclear as to what type of homeless shelters and what kind of perceptions.
>
> Let's rewrite it in a clearer manner: "The purpose of my study was to investigate how of mothers of birth to one year children perceive full-services assistance provided by homeless shelters in a major urban U.S. city." That is better because we know the topic and the measurable component which is "perceptions of full-services assistance."

> *Example 2.* "The study focuses on co-teaching." Here is a critique of this purpose statement. First, it is better if you use first person because the reader will know "whose" study it is.
>
> This statement may follow text in which you have just discussed a study about co-teaching. With the statement of "The study focuses on co-teaching, or therefore, the study focuses on co-teaching," it is unclear as to if it is your study or the other study that discussed co-teaching.
>
> We would change your purpose to begin—"My study." Since you have already completed the study or will have by the end of the course, you would want to put your verb in past tense—"My study focused on …"

Use the Formula

It is much better if you use our formula and begin your purpose statement as such—"The purpose of my study was to…." Let's consider Example 2 purpose statement.

Are the measurable components clear in the original statement? No; therefore, we would suggest, "The purpose of my study was to conduct a cross-case analysis of co-teaching in social studies from the perspectives of first-year teachers in five exemplary middle schools in Mississippi." From that statement, clarity is developed by naming the type of study and the measured components of – (a) co-teaching, (b) social studies, (c) first-year teachers, and (d) five exemplary middle schools in Mississippi.

> *Example 3.* "Additionally, my study investigated the perspective of my own personal experience as a leader, as well as the perspective of two other leaders' perspectives on implementing a prekindergarten Montessori bilingual program" (Rodriguez, 2002, p. iv).
>
> This is a slightly different way to write the purpose statement when personal narrative and reflection are involved as a primary source. All components are found in this statement. The topic is about the implementation and maintenance of prekindergarten Montessori bilingual programs and leadership. The components to be measured are leaders' perspectives on that implementation and maintenance of their programs.

Concluding Thoughts

The purpose statement in qualitative research is important to you as it aids in giving you direction and keeping you on track. It is important for your readers because it basically outlines the direction you took as you investigated your topic. The purpose statement, as the advanced organizer for your study, guides the readers in their expectations of the research manuscript, article, or report.

According to Cresswell (1998), a more definitive explanation of your purpose may follow the actual purpose statement. You may follow the general purpose statement, using the example above about bilingual parents and their children's literacy with: "In this phenomenological study, I defined bilingual children as those who speak Spanish as their native language and who are learning English in school. Specifically, literacy was defined as oral language development in Spanish and English."

The purpose statement is sometimes placed at the very beginning of the introduction to a manuscript, but often you will see it placed at the ending of the introduction, problem, and significance. Generally, the problem should lead the reader into the purpose of the study.

Target Activities

Target 2.   Develop Your Purpose

A. Congratulations—you are right on target. It is now time for you to write your purpose statement. First, you will need to practice writing your purpose. Complete one or both of the activities of webbing or sticky notes. Practice getting your purpose to the specificity it needs.

Purpose Draft 1:

_____

_____

Purpose Draft 2: (Here you will refine your first draft.)

_____

_____

Purpose Draft 3: (Reread the purpose statement again aloud. Does it contain all the parts as discussed earlier? Is it clear? If a reader picked up your purpose statement, would the reader understand exactly what you did in your study?)

_____

_____

Remember, you will want to begin your purpose statement—**The purpose of my study is to... (for the proposal). If you are completing your dissertation—you will write—The purpose of my study was to...**

B. Rewrite these purpose statements using the formula and the components of the purpose. (Note: In scholarly writing, we would not advise using the terms "look at" or "find out.")

Purpose 1: The purpose was to look at differences between certified and non-certified teachers.

_____

_____

Purpose 2: I wanted to find out whether women principals thought differently about social justice as opposed to male principals.

_____

_____

Purpose 3: The purpose of my study was to determine what assimilation problems first-year teachers have.

_____

_____

References

Bogdan, R.C., & Biklen, S.K. (2007). *Qualitative research for education*. Boston, MA: Pearson Education, Inc.

Creswell, J. (1998). *Qualitative inquiry and research design: Choosing among five traditions.* London, New Delhi, Thousand Oaks, Sage Publications.

Rodriguez, R. (2002). An analysis of a public school prekindergarten Montessori bilingual program. Dissertation Abstract International. DAI 63 (07), p. 2429. Retrieved on October 20, 2006 from http://proquest.umi.com.unx1.shsu.edu:2048/pqdweb?index=0&did=764691811& SrchMode=1&sid=1&Fmt=2&VInst=PROD&VType=PQD&RQT=309&VName =PQD&TS=1171542040&clientId=96

TIP #3 DEVELOP YOUR INTRODUCTION, REVIEW OF LITERATURE, AND PROBLEM

By this time in your graduate program you must have written several reviews of literature for various courses. We must qualify Tip #3 for qualitative research. Some of our colleagues believe that the review of literature should not be completed until the study has actually been underway and emerging themes are beginning to be processed by the researcher. Nonetheless, we are attempting to assist you via this manual to complete your research study within the semester; therefore, we will discuss how to complete this section of the study and how to write it in a timely manner.

The process for completing this section which is the introduction to your study is like a formulaic funnel. The funnel begins with a brief review of literature on the broad topic of your paper with a few points that will draw in the reader into your study. Then, the funnel narrows and continues to narrow as you, the researcher, bring the reader to the main problem of your study.

In this section, we advocate actually blending your introduction and review of literature and funneling down to your problem. This is the "why" of your interest in the topic.

Just as you thought about your topic and brainstormed ideas, it is also important to do the same in this portion of the study. First we know that you have been reading the literature and determining what are the critical issues within your area of interest. This part of the writing can be one of the most enjoyable if you have a map of where you need to go. Let's begin developing such a map.

Step 1: Create a Map

The introductory component of your qualitative paper is extremely important to your study. It tells the reader critcal information about your topic. How do you determine what is to be in this introductory section of the research paper? Remember, you will begin in a general format and then move to more specific information. First, before a map is created, you will need to go back to your purpose statement. The purpose statement is the pinpoint on your map. It steers you in the right direction.

Let's examine a purpose statement of two of our former doctoral students, who worked as a research team and were successful in getting their research study published.

> The purpose of this study was to determine whether the location of dual enrollment courses on the high school or college campus affected the educational experience of dual enrollment students. Because most community colleges encourage high school students to co-enroll in college classes for credit, dual enrollment is one of the fastest growing services offered by community colleges. Both high schools and the colleges benefit from these dual enrollment arrangements. High school students can complete some of their college core curriculum before they graduate from high school, and the college benefits immediately from increased revenue while building a student base in the area. A high school student who is co-enrolled in college classes is likely to attend that community college after high school graduation. (Burns & Lewis, 2000, ¶ 11)

In the introduction and review of related literature you will find the topics that are highlighted in the excerpt of the purpose statement above. Lewis and Burns (see Lewis and Burns, 2000) began their research article with a general overview of dual enrollment programs. Then they moved to the current state of dual enrollment and placement where some problems were brought to the reader's attention and then wrote about the educational experience of quality of such programs for the students enrolled in such programs. Next they spoke to the specific concerns about dual enrollment and then discussed the climate of dual enrollment programs from the study perspective. In the final portion of their review of literature within the introduction, they turned the focus back to proximity of dual enrollment programs for students. The highlighted areas in the purpose statement definitely were addressed: (a) dual enrollment, (b) students in such programs, and (c) educational experiences related to dual enrollment. Their purpose gave them the initial steps for their map.

Step 2: **Design a Web for Your Review of Literature**

From the purpose statement, you may wish to create a webbed review of literature activity by taking your own prior knowledge and some of the literature that you have read on your topic already. Let's take the Lewis and Burns example. Figure 3.1 demonstrates what they might have developed as a webbed activity.

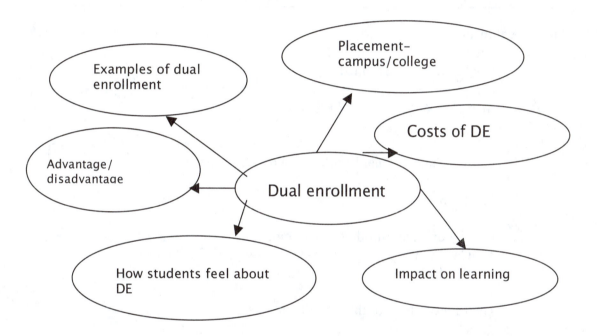

Figure 3.1 *Web that demonstrates thought from purpose statement to introduction and review of literature.*

From the web, an outline can be developed. Here you can get even more specific. You want to be as fluent as possible as you develop your outline. As you see in the webbed activity for the review of literature, we start with dual enrollment at the center. Things that may impact dual enrollment or thing that may be of interest to review in terms of previous research and publications are: (a) examples of dual enrollment, (b) placement of the dual enrollment programs—either on college or the high school campus, (c) costs of dual enrollment, (d) advantages and disadvantages of dual enrollment, (e) how students feel about dual enrollment, and (f) the impact dual enrollment might have on learning. Those were all considered to be important in having the background related to this study.

The next step would be to outline the topics. How would you think these topics might fit together in a review of literature for the introduction of your paper and how might this provide the reader with the significant problem you want to address? An initial outline for the topic of dual enrollment might look like the one in Table 3.1.

Table 3.1

Initial Outline for Review of Literature for the Topic of Dual Enrollment

Dual Enrollment

    I.   Dual Enrollment Defined

    II.   Size of Dual Enrollment Programs

    III.   Current State of Dual Enrollment Programs
        a. Accountability
        b. Types

    IV.   Quality of Dual Enrollment Programs
        a. Community Colleges and University Transfer Policies
        b. Problems

    V.   Dual Enrollment for the Traditional Leaner

    VI.   Problems with Dual Enrollment

    VII.   Dual Enrollment and Climate

Step 3: Get the Information for the Literature Review and Begin Writing

The introduction and review of literature serve four purposes:

1.   to survey what has been studied and recommended related to your topic both quantitatively and qualitatively,
2.   to gain a better understanding of the problems and issues surrounding your topic,
3.   to study research designs, procedures, and instruments used in quantitative and qualitative research that might assist in designing your own research, procedures, and instruments, and
4.   to review limitations addressed in previous studies so that you will not repeat those in your related study.

The more you know about your topic, the better the review of literature, the introduction to your paper, and the better you can get the problem with which you are concerned across to your reader. You may know a great deal about your topic, but there may have been very few research studies published about it. Therefore, it is incumbent upon you to review "related" literature surrounding your topic.

There are eight considerations as you begin writing your introduction, review of literature, and problem.

Consideration 1. Documents to Search

Look back at your outline or the web you developed on your review of literature. That is where you should begin your search of documents which should include published articles, encyclopedias and handbooks of the field, abstracts, book reviews, books, annual research reviews, monographs, dissertations, theses, government reports, research reports, documentaries (if related to the topic), blogs, and wikis. Even though we do not particularly advocate including editorialized personal opinions that may be included in blogs or wikis, the point here is that a quick qualitative review of conversations and postings in such locations could aid your search from a public perception point of view.

Consideration 2. Visit the Librarian

A trip to the university library and a meeting with one of the reference librarians can save you a lot of time and energy. Ask the librarian the following questions:

1.   What references are available in the library?
2.   What references are available to me online?
3.   Is there a special code or way in which I must access information online?

4.   How to obtain dissertations or theses I need to review? Is there any charge?

5.   If I can't find an article, how do I go about getting a copy? Is there any charge?

6.   Is there someone here who can help me via online chat? Via personal meetings?

7.   How can I obtain a copy of a specific encyclopedia such as the *Encyclopedia of Special Education, A Reference for the Education of Children, Adolescents, and Adults with Disabilities and Other Exceptional Individuals, Volume 2, Third Edition* edited by Fletcher-Janzen & Reynolds in 2007?

8.   How can I find a variety of sources related to the types of documents we have suggested to review in Step 1?

9.   Ask the reference librarian to assist you developing a list of search words or terms that would help in facilitating your review of literature.

You will want to get as much information from the librarian as soon as possible to that if you must order any materials for your research study for the semester. You see by doing this, you will have already attacked that issue early in the semester. This exercise will be great practice for when you begin your dissertation work.

Consideration 3. Determine Your Sources

After you have met with the librarian and she/he has assisted you in determining key words and how you might obtain materials, you are prepared now to decide what sources you will use. Remember, you will want to use primary sources to report in the literature unless a secondary source is written by an individual with great credibility and a depth of background on the topic.

Use primary sources in most cases.

For example, you may review something in a handbook, which would be more than likely a secondary source, that an expert has developed based on an extensive review of literature, a best evidence synthesis, or a meta-analysis.

You might use a secondary source to get an overview of your topic, or you might use a secondary source to even expand your review of literature. It could expand the literature review in the regard that perhaps new avenues are presented on the topic, or it could even serve to narrow the literature review in that the topic may have already been studied in depth on the issue in which you are interested. If you are citing legislation, report the actual bill, act, or amendment.

Always check the primary source.

The importance of primary sources can be explained by this true story. Recently, one of the professors indicated to us that he was reviewing a manuscript for a journal, and he came across a reference of his own. However, to his surprise, he could not remember stating what the author had indicated in the sentence.

As a result, he called the editor who suggested he contact the author. He did so, and lo and behold, the author had not gone to the original, primary source of the professor's original work; rather, the author had taken that information from a secondary source—that was wrong. So, the moral of this story is—be certain to review the primary source.

Consideration 4. Search for Literature

The librarian should have provided you with some particular databases to search for your topic. Of course, you would use the library's catalogue for particular books. We suggest you also search for books at such sites as: Amazon.com, Barnes and Noble.com, Bordersbooks.com, ebay.com, Halfpricebooks.com, or Hastings.com. If your library does not have the book, perhaps you could obtain it through interlibrary loan or even purchase an inexpensive used copy online or through your campus bookstore.

> There is a program that to which most of the university libraries belong. For example, in Texas, that is TEXSHARE. Upon signing up for a TEXSHARE card at most Texas university libraries, the student or faculty member is free to go to the participating university libraries and check out books. Prior to reviewing the literature in books available at the library or other libraries or via interlibrary loan, you may want to invest in a handheld scanner which can scan only the pages you need. This will not only help you in organizing the text material, but it will also save your back from having to carry all those heavy books.

> You will want to search your key terms via such search engines and databases as: Academic Premier Host, America's Newspapers, ArticleFIRST, ProQuest, EBSCO Host, Education Full Text, Emerald Full Text, First Gov, Humanities Full Text , Ingenta, JSTOR, LexisNexis Academic, Project MUSE, Wilson OmniFile Full Text, or WorldCat. Your university library will likely own rights to most of those particular databases. Other databases that many of our students have found helpful are: edweek.org; ed.gov/NCES; wwwcsteep.bc.edu; ed.gov; and Questia.com.

> Be certain to make a note where you found your literature as you begin printing it out. Sometimes the printer will include the database and URL, but sometimes it does not. Also, be certain your copied articles and facts have the proper citations attached or written on them. Make a note at the time as to whether it is research based or opinion. The problem is that you can lose reference citations and waste time looking and looking for them..

Consideration 5. Evaluate the Literature

Now that you have reviewed all the literature and printed or copied articles, portions of books, etc., you must evaluate what you have. Remember, your best sources are the primary ones.

Additionally, you will want to review the literature you have with the following things in mind: (a) what is the age of the material; if it is an older piece of work, does it lend to the study historically or to a trend?; (b) where did you find your source?; look for your citation—was it on someone's website who was simply stating his/her opinion, or was it reported in a major research paper published in a refereed journal; if it is opinion, is it someone who is well known in the field and is quotable?; (c) what is the relationship of the information found in each item found to your topic?; (d) does the research you have found have methodological flaws; (e) is the book a reprint?; has it been updated?, and (f) does the material you found support or refute other citations you have already determined important to your study?

Consideration 6. Organize your Findings

Now, you will want to review your findings and lay it out according to the outline. These actions are actually a part of qualitative research in that this is the point where you will conduct a document analysis based on the predetermined "themes" in your outline. Put the pieces of literature together in this order. If several pieces of literature relate to each other, either in a supportive or contradictory way, put those together with a paper clip.

As you are rereading those papers and articles, you will want to make notes on the copies. This will remind you of important points you want to emphasis when you begin to write.

Consideration 7. Begin to Write

It is important to begin to write as soon as you are organized. Remember the funnel approach to this section. Remember, you are introducing the topic, providing supportive documentation through the literature, and bringing the reader right down to the problem.

As you write you will want to cluster studies that have related findings. For example if independent studies come to similar conclusions you can simply state the conclusion and reference that conclusion with all studies reported in the parenthetical reference list in the text. For example, the American Psychological Association's (APA' 2001) *Publication Manual* provided the following as a model: "People whose occupations require great analytical skill produce less alpha activity than those whose occupations do not require such analytical skill (Doktor & Bloom, 1977; Ornstein & Galin, 1976)" (p.307). Note similar findings were determined to exist in these two independent research studies; therefore, APA style suggests that two studies be combined.

If you find studies that are contradictory, you will need to report these. You will not want to report *only* studies that support your particular point of view. Additionally, you will not want to report *only* qualitative studies for your qualitative research report; rather, include all relevant research. We provide a good sample from a recent journal article by Barrerra (2006) related to contradictory, clarifying, or opposing statements:

> The process of learning a second language is itself one that takes place in phases, initially for basic communication, and subsequently for academic learning proficiency only after several years (Baca & Cervantes, 1991; Cummins, 1989; Skutnabb-Kangas, 1984). This process is expected to take place at a certain pace-1 to 2 years for basic communication, and 5 to 7 years for academic language. However, such progress is contingent on a strongly literate background in the learner's first language (Cummins, 1989; Krashen, 1998,1981), without which one can expect an even longer period before developing the ability to use English for

academic learning (Collier & Thomas, 1995; Greene, 1997; Thomas & Collier, 1997). (p. 143)

The problem and significance of the study can sometimes be one and the same. The problem will tell the reader the main issue(s) related to your topic. For example, sometimes there may have been quantitative studies on the topic, but no qualitative work discussing the intricacies of the topic to better understand it has been conducted. That may be a legitimate problem to report, but it is also related to the significance of the research as well. Sometimes the problem is inherent in the literature review and is written into the review itself. The significance, as well as the problem, get to the point of the "why" of the study. Why is this study important? Why is what I want to study a contributor to the understanding of a phenomenon or an event or an educational issue?

Consideration 8. Check your Writing

It is critical to check your work. Our recommendation is first to edit, second to edit, third to edit, fourth to edit, fifth to edit, and sixth to edit. Prior to submitting anything to your professor, it is good that you have edited and rewritten at least six times. Additionally, it is good to submit your work, once you have completed your sixth edit, to your university writing center or to a knowledgeable person in grammar, punctuation, and whatever style manual your professor is requiring.

Our final word of wisdom on this section is to ensure that that you have not plagiarized. Many university professors either allow students to use or they use a service called turnitin.com which checks all over the Internet and with papers that have been previously submitted for plagiarized text. I knew of a professor once who had a paper turned in with over 79% of the paper copied. That is a tragedy and can lead to an expulsion from the graduate program. Plagiarism is a serious offense. The best bet to counter plagiarism is to write the findings in your own words and then give the appropriate citation or reference according to the style manual you are using. If you want, you may quote the author(s) directly-- again, providing the appropriate citation with page numbers. APA (2001; p. 349) provided the following example as a paraphrased example of what was written in their actual text of the manual:

> As stated in the fifth edition of the *Publication Manual of the American Psychological Association*, the ethical principles of scientific publication are designed to ensure the integrity of scientific knowledge and to protect the intellectual property rights of others….

In this example, APA provided the source as the fifth edition of the *Publication Manual of the American Psychological Association*. Had the statement been written as—The ethical principles of scientific publications are designed to ensure the integrity of scientific knowledge and to protect the property rights of others, and that had been written without providing a reference even though it is paraphrased, it is plagiarized. Besides, a reader would wonder how the author would have known that or where he/she would have gotten that information.

Target Activities

Target 3. Develop Your Introduction, Review of Literature, and Problem

A. Sometimes the problem and significance can be written in one section, because sometimes the problem becomes the significance of the study. In the following example, a paper published from a qualitative research class we taught, Burns and Lewis (2000) began their research manuscript, and subsequently their article, broadly and brought the study down to the problem. As you can see, they included their purpose and significance statements together and did not have a separate header of problem as the significance in this study was the problem. Look at the structure of this introduction and purpose and the flow of the beginning of the paper. See how this section sets the tone for the remainder of what is to come.

Introduction

Dual enrollment is difficult to define for many reasons. Virtually every state has high schools and colleges that work within the framework of a dual enrollment system. Additionally, the very definition of dual enrollment is extremely broad. This phenomenon can most probably be attributed to the fact that there are many uses and objectives associated with dual enrollment. In its most simple form, dual enrollment is a system of cooperation between a high school and a university or community college that allows a student to attain college credit while pursuing a high school diploma; however, dual enrollment has evolved into much more (Fincher-Ford, 1996; School-to-Work, 1997). More precisely, the School-to-Work Glossary of Terms (1997) defined dual enrollment as, "…a program of study allowing high school students to simultaneously earn credits toward a high school diploma and a post secondary degree or certificate" (p. 25).

Dual enrollment programs may be very small, involving a cooperation between one high school and one community college. Dual enrollment programs may also be very large, involving a cooperation between a community college and many schools in various counties. Very large programs such as this one usually serve a very large area and a very diverse student population (Delaino, 1990). Despite the fact that dual enrollment programs vary greatly in size, purpose, goals, mission, and population, served all have one thing in common. Dual enrollment programs exist to meet the specific needs of the high school students they serve (Galloway, 1994).

Current State of Dual Enrollment

Despite the fact that the number of dual enrollment programs in the United States is currently very high, this is a critical time for dual enrollment. States, community colleges, and high schools are more aware of fiscal accountability than ever before; hence, program scrutiny is at an all time high. Any program that does not have clearly articulated objectives, methods for reaching those objectives, and data to support progress is in jeopardy of being cut. Dual enrollment programs are not exempt from this accountability. The diverse functions and purposes of dual enrollment programs in this country offers evidence to the flexibility of dual enrollment programs on the whole; however, this makes accountability somewhat difficult. Each program must have unique performance objectives and a data driven method to measure progress towards those objectives. For example, vocational preparedness is a goal of many dual enrollment programs in this country; hence, a dual enrollment program focused on preparedness must be capable of showing evidence of a smoother transition for high school students in the program to the workforce (Accountability/Flexibility, 1990; Running Start, 1997).

Transferability and Quality of Education

It is not enough for a student to have the option to take high school and college courses for simultaneous credit; the credit must count for something. Of course, virtually no problem exists concerning the involved high school accepting the dual enrollment hours for credit; however, the transferability of the courses to a different community college or university is sometimes a difficult issue. When a dual credit agreement is reached between a high school and a community college, there is seldom an issue of transferability between those two institutions. The problem occurs when the student attempts to transfer the credit hours to a university or college that was not involved in the dual credit agreement. Ultimately, the student is at the mercy of the institution to which they are transferring. For example, the University of Florida does not accept dual enrollment chemistry hours from any college or university unless the student meets standard admissions requirements. As in any transfer, this decision is well within the jurisdiction of the University of Florida. Any university, ultimately, will have the final decision pertaining to transferability, whether the hours are dual enrollment hours or not (Brown, 1993; Windham, 1997).

Dual Enrollment for the Traditional Learner

Contrary to popular belief, dual enrollment is not exclusively for the academically gifted learner. There are many dual enrollment programs that target the lesser-gifted student. South Dakota public schools used dual enrollment as a tool to decrease the drop out rate of their high-risk students. Often at risk students do not see the purpose of attending school. The perception is that there is very little practical application for a person that does not aspire to go to college. South Dakota utilized dual enrollment to teach students vocational skills, to spark an interest in academics and to try to teach the students better learning strategies (Hoachlander & Tuma, 1989; Haas, 1990).

Many non-gifted students are capable of having success in college; however, they often have trouble in the transition from high school to college. Some dual enrollment programs are focused primarily on aiding an average student in making this difficult transition (The Continuum, 1992). Some students simply will not have success in the traditional education system of our country. Unless they are given an opportunity to learn job skills and ways to have success in the American workforce, they are destined to fail in life. Traditional high schools often fail in preparing these students. Dual enrollment programs gives them a chance at success (Galloway, 1994).

Promoting cultural pride and acceptance of diversity is another purpose of some non-academic based dual enrollment programs. David E. Bogert (1995) described a community college system in Florida focused on bettering students academically, increasing cultural awareness and acceptance and granting dual credit for high school and college. Many primarily minority districts are utilizing dual enrollment to better prepare students for a success transition into college or the workforce (Chatel & Cimochowski, 1997).

Problems with Dual Enrollment

Although there are many advantages to the dual enrollment system, there are some drawbacks. Many courses do not meet the specific needs of the students they are supposed to serve. For example, a course may not be rigorous enough for a gifted student and too rigorous for a non-gifted student. Transportation to the site where the courses are offered and transferability of hours post graduation are also potential problems with a dual enrollment program (Reiss & Follo, 1993).

Cost is another potential drawback to the dual enrollment system. The method of funding dual enrollment varies greatly. For some, the cost falls directly to the student and his or her family. In other instances, it is subsidized in part or whole by the state. Some colleges offer scholarships and other forms of aid to entice students to enter a dual enrollment program (Fincher-Ford, 1996).

Dual Enrollment and Climate

School climate undoubtedly has a significant impact on student learning. School climate is simply the atmosphere and morale in a particular school. There has been no research conducted specifically on the impact of climate on co-enrollment. This fact can most probably be attributed to the fact that dual enrollment is only now becoming a readily accepted and even expected part of high school curriculum. There are an infinite number factors that contribute to the climate of a school. Howard, Howell, and Brainard (1987) argued that proximity and school facilities contribute greatly to climate; hence, there are clear climate implications that should be considered when selecting which facility to use for a dual enrollment course, the college or high school.

Purpose and Significance of the Study

The purpose of this study was to determine whether the location of dual enrollment courses on the high school or college campus affected the educational experience of dual enrollment students. Because most community colleges encourage high school students to co-enroll in college classes for credit, dual enrollment is one of the fastest growing services offered by community colleges. Both high schools and the colleges benefit from these dual enrollment arrangements. High school students can complete some of their college core curriculum before they graduate from high school, and the college benefits immediately from increased revenue while building a student base in the area. A high school student who is co-enrolled in college classes is likely to attend that community college after high school graduation.

The study focused on the effect of location of those classes. In some community colleges, the college instructor travels to the high school, usually one evening a week, to teach the class in that environment. In some cases, the college class is limited to current high school students and is offered during the regular school day. Usually these classes are taught by a regular high school faculty member who is working as an adjunct community college instructor. In other situations, the co-enrolled students come to the college campus. At a time when all educational institutions are trying to offer more opportunity for students with fewer resources, administrators have to be concerned about offering the choices that allow the student to complete his or her goals. If one location (either the high school or college campus) proves to be more conducive for the success of the college student, this would allow administrators to make wiser course scheduling decisions.

> *Taken from Dual-Enrolled Students' Perceptions of the Effect of Classroom Environment on Educational Experience by Heath Burns and Beth Lewis. The Qualitative Report, Volume 4, Numbers 1 & 2, January, 2000 (http://www.nova.edu/ssss/QR/QR4-1/burns.html)*

B. Share with a fellow student another article you find and analyze the structure of the research article in the initial part of the paper.

1. Where is the introduction?

2. Is problem considered within the introduction?

3. Where is the purpose placed?

4. Is significance a part of the problem or purpose?

5. Is there a separate review of literature section?

6. How fast does the author get you to the problem and purpose of the study? Do you have to read and read to find it?

References

American Psychological Association. (2001). *Publication manual of the American psychological association: Fifth edition.* Washington, D.C.: Author.

Barrera, M. Roles of definitional and assessment models in the identification of new or second language learners of English for special education. *Journal of Learning Disabilities* v. 39(2). 142-156.

Bogdan, R.C., & Biklen, S.K. (2007). *Qualitative research for education.* Boston, MA: Pearson Education, Inc.

Lewis, B., & Burns, H. (2000). Dual-enrolled students' perceptions of the effect of classroom environment on educational experience. *The Qualitative Report, 4*(1&2). Retrieved on October 14, 2006 from http://www.nova.edu/ssss/QR/QR4-1/burns.html.

Miles, M.B., & Huberman, A.M. (1994). *Qualitative data analysis.* Thousand Oaks, CA: Sage

TIP #4 DETERMINE YOUR THEORETICAL FRAMEWORK

You have been reviewing the literature, reading, and you have begun to write. You know your purpose. Now it is time for you to determine what theory(ies) will guide your research or if you will have a theoretical framework in your study. The theoretical framework is much like the frame of a house. It is the body, the glue, the component that holds the house together. It

is the foundation that gives the house shape. That is similar to a theoretical framework. We will share with you what a theoretical framework is and how you might utilize one in your study.

Step 1: **Review the Definition of Theoretical Framework**

We define a theoretical framework as a guiding theory or combination of theories that aid in giving direction to the study. The theoretical framework is seen throughout the study, grounding it, framing it, giving it direction, and bringing it to closure. If a specific theory cannot be found, then the theoretical framework may be offered as the review of literature itself. Whatever is the case—specific theory or literature—it should be knowledge-based, coherent, and consistent with the topic or phenomenon under study, and you should continuously consider and reflect upon during your study. As a result, your theoretical framework will help to distinguish your study from among others related to the topic you selected

May (1999), while discussing women's studies, indicated "…a strong theoretical framework is requisite. Without theory, students' preconceived notions about knowledge and subjectivity as transparent, immediate, and unified are left unchallenged, and yet these preconceived, taken-for-granted notions undergird the social practices and beliefs…" (p. 25).

You may see theoretical framework referred to as conceptual framework. For example, Miles and Huberman (1994) used the term, "conceptual

> *Sometimes, the theoretical framework is also noted as the conceptual framework.*

framework," in place of theoretical framework and stated, "A conceptual framework explains, either graphically or in narrative form, the main things to be studied—the key factors, constructs or variables—and the presumed relationships among them" (p. 18).

How the Theoretical Framework is Used

There are a couple of ways in which the theoretical framework can be used: (a) for initial or preliminary understanding and guidance, (b) for serving as a basis for validation of the theory itself via the data collected and analyzed, and (c) for guiding the research throughout the study and explication of the data.

Initial understanding and guidance. The theoretical framework can be used for initial guidance for your research. For example, Audet and Amboise (2001) indicated such in their research

> The theoretical framework was essentially preliminary: it was to be used as a starting point for investigation, as guidance for the first steps in the field. It was never meant to preclude from investigating other variables of interest that were brought into attention while collecting data in the field. It was understood that such framework was to be modified as needed, to fit with empirical findings that were likely to emerge from the field. It is in that sense that our approach was inductive and aimed at theory building. (¶ 8)

Yin (1993) indicated that a theory could actually provide guidance to the researcher, when working within a case study design, in better defining the inquiry and making if more effective.

Serving as a basis for validation of the theory itself. Validation of the theory used as the theoretical framework is acceptable within the qualitative research paradigm. For example, Schlosberg's (2003) study, *An International Case Study: The Transportability of the Synergistic Leadership Theory to Selected Educational Leaders in Mexico*, used the Synergistic Leadership Theory (Irby, Brown, Duffy, & Trautman, 2000) as the theoretical framework, but also validated the theory across cultures.

Guiding the research throughout the study and explication of the data. Gall, Gall, and Borg (2000) provided a definition of theory: "an explanation of a certain set of observed phenomena in terms of a system of constructs and laws that relate these constructs to each other" (p.8). Accordingly, a theory is a systematic explanatory statement of some phenomena, ranging from simple generalizations to a complex set of laws (Lunenburg & Ornstein, 2000; Patterson, 1986). The laws of theory enable us to make predictions and to control phenomena. Theories provide a guiding framework that allows predicting what should be observable where data are not already available (Lunenburg & Ornstein).

Step 2: **Determine Your Theoretical Framework**

First, look at your topic. Reflect upon the topic and read, read, read. Answering the following questions is a first step in determining your framework.

1. What are key terms that come up over and over in your readings (readings of journals, books, and dissertations)?

2. What are dispositions that support your topic?

3. What are theories that have been developed about your topic by others?

4. Are there diversity issues related to your topic as a basis for the theory?

Step 3: **Refine Your Theoretical Framework**

Once you have determined there are one, two, or three theories that support your topic, then you will need to decide which will be placed and explained first, second, then third. Reflect about the theory(ies) throughout the study and determine how, if there is more than one, that it will be integrated into the explication of the findings.

In this step, you will determine whether your review of literature will need to serve as the theoretical framework, because sometimes there is no specific theory that is directly related to the topic of study.

Target Activities

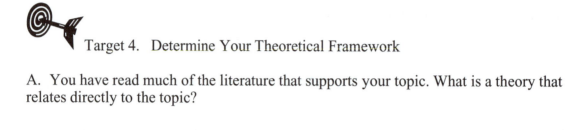

Target 4.   Determine Your Theoretical Framework

A. You have read much of the literature that supports your topic. What is a theory that relates directly to the topic?

_____

_____

_____

_____

B. Following is an example of a Theoretical Framework. This example would be what is expected of you given your current level of experience and expertise. This theoretical framework was written by Marilyn Butler, doctoral student, Sam Houston State University, and it appears after the introduction, purpose, and significance of the study; presented here is a sample of her proposed purpose, significance and theoretical framework.

> The purpose of my study is to measure the impact of a leadership intervention on Latina high school students' self-esteem, leadership behaviors, and career aspirations.
>
> ### Significance of the Study
>
> The Hispanic population of the US increased from 2000 to 2005 by 22%. In the US, there are more than 21 nations considered to be of Hispanic origin. The top five countries of Hispanic origin are: Mexico, 64%; Puerto Rico, 9.1%; Cuba, 3.5%; Salvador, 3.0%, and Dominican Republic, 2.7%. In Texas, 74% of the Hispanic population originates from Mexico (Pew Hispanic Center, 2006; Murdock, 2005). The increase of the Hispanic population in Texas is attributed to natural growth, births, migration, and immigration. The average age of native born Hispanics is 27 years compared to the average age of native born Whites which is 40 (The Pew Hispanic Center, 2006). The largest segment of the growing native born Hispanic population is birth to four years of age (Pew Hispanic Center; US Census 2006). Two-thirds of the US Hispanic population in 2005 over the age of 25 has an educational attainment of

high school graduation or less (The Pew Hispanic Center). The average annual income of Hispanic population in Texas is $29,873 (The Pew Institute, 2004). Based on income quintile, the Hispanic population falls into the second quintile (US Census Bureau, 2003). The rapid growth in population will lead to a younger, poorer and less educated population (Petersen, 2005). The tax base of Texas will be reduced due to a larger population of lower income workers (US Census, 2006). This will be combined with greater demands on all the state welfare systems, especially the educational system and the health care system. As educational attainment improves workforce attainment will increase (Closing the Gap, 2005). Workforce attainment will improve the economic status by moving from a lower quintile to a higher quintile, into the middle class (US Census, 2006). A larger middle class will lead to a broader tax base (Closing the Gap). One only needs to look at the pattern set by California to see the results of a rapidly growing ethnic population. The need to educate the changing population of Texas and prepare them for leadership is a major concern for the entire state (Closing the Gap, 2005).

A recent study about youth behavior by Moore and Zaff (2002), indicated in their research that positive as well as negative behavior among cluster groups of youth has a domino effect. The researchers recommended that youth programs should engage the youth while they are young and malleable in order to have the greatest positive impact. The intent is to work with positive behaviors to circumvent the negative behaviors (Moore & Zaff, 2002). The report also states that teens who participate in community service activities are more successful in school, are more stable emotionally, and possess better social skills (Moore & Zaff, 2002).

This was substantiated by the longitudinal study at the University of California at Los Angeles (UCLA) through the Cooperative Institute Research Program (CIRP). Sax (2000) reports about the freshman college student and from the longitudinal study reports on the same college freshman 10 years later. The students that participated in community service in high school were not only more successful in college but also in the workplace (Sax, 2000).

In youth programs across America, the Positive Youth Development Movement is affecting the mission, goals and programs of leading youth organizations. "The focus of the movement is to develop or enhance individual and environmental assets" (Fisher, Imm, Chinman, & Wandersman, 2006, p. x). The *40 Developmental Assets for Adolescents* were developed by *The Search Institute*, an independent, nonprofit organization, to promote healthy children, youth, and communities. They have identified the "building blocks of healthy development that help young people grow up healthy, caring, and responsible" (p. xx). The Assets are being integrated into the programs of youth organizations.

Girl Scouts is a service based, pluralistic, leadership oriented organization (GSUSA, 2006). The Girl Scout organization has touched the lives of women across cultures and time. Research conducted by the organization about women and families in today's society is very instructive. In a recent study of a cross-section of American women it was determined that regardless of socio-economic condition, educational attainment, or marital status, the most valued things in life in terms of "achieving success" was "individual well being and personal relationships" (GSUSA, 1999, p.6).

Theoretical Framework

Theories are simplified models of complex relationships functioning as a lens through which situations are viewed. The theoretical framework for my study originated in a book written by Helen Astin and Carole Leland (1991), *Women of Vision, Women of Influence: A Cross-Generational Study of Leaders and Social Change*. The book tells the story of three generations of female leaders who worked to make a difference in education and public service. In the book, it is the accomplishment of the leader rather than the position that is emphasized. Leadership is viewed as a cooperative effort of empowerment.

The three groups of women identified by Astin and Leland were: predecessors, instigators, and inheritors. Predecessors were women who matured between the post World War I and pre-Great Depression Era. They believed that education was essential to improving the lives of women. Instigators were women who assumed highly visible roles of leadership and were seen as agents of change from 1960 to 1970 during the height of the Feminist Movement. Inheritors were the group of women who benefited from and were changed by the actions of the Instigators (Astin, 1991, p.xvii). They assumed leadership roles across the nation repeating the process.

The Astin Model of Predecessor, Instigator, and Inheritor was foundational in developing the Astin *Social Change Model* (SCM), (Astin, 1999). The model incorporates a set of leadership development values that assume all student are possible leaders. There are seven core values of the model grouped into three domains: a) Individual values, including consciousness of self, congruence, and commitment; b) group values, including collaboration, common purpose, and controversy with civility; c) community values including citizenship (Outcalt, Farris, & McMahon, p.181, 1999).

There are three objective of the SCM are to: a) increase knowledge of self through reflection and active participation, b) increase leadership competency, and c) be positive agent of social change. The SCM is illustrated in Figure 1 as a Venn diagram. The framework for the study will be the original Astin Model of Predecessor, Instigator, and Inheritor. Women from the community will be identified and utilized as role models and mentors in the leadership intervention. The theoretical frame for the leadership intervention will be the SCM (Astin, p.7, 1996; Outcalt, Farris, & McMahon, p.182, 1999).

Figure 1. The Social Change Model: the individual domain, the group domain, and the community domain (Astin, 2001)

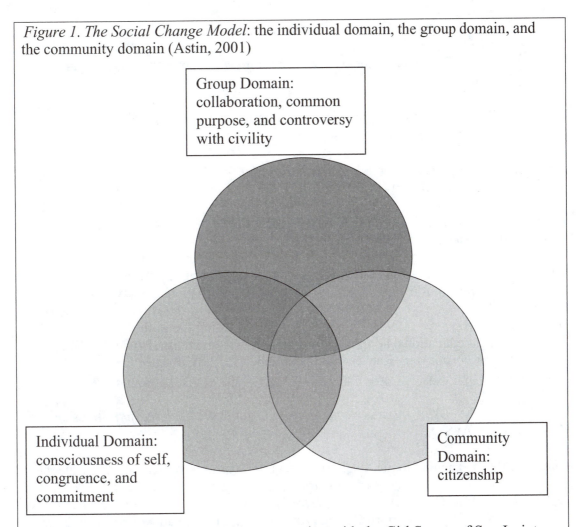

Group Domain: collaboration, common purpose, and controversy with civility

Individual Domain: consciousness of self, congruence, and commitment

Community Domain: citizenship

My study will be conducted in cooperation with the Girl Scouts of San Jacinto Council (GSSJC) in Houston, Texas. GSSJC serves a diverse population spanning more than 23 counties in southeast Texas including the major metropolitan area of Houston. *Latinas Taking the Lead* is an initiative of the Pluralism Committee of GSSJC. The leadership model for Girl Scouts is consistent with the Astin Model of Predecessor, Instigator, and Inheritor.

In Girl Scouting, leadership is also viewed as a cooperative effort of empowerment among women at various stages of life. Girl Scouts has developed a leadership development program that begins at age five and continues through high school into adulthood. The Girl Scout leadership program of advisor and scout will be part of the theoretical framework as the roles of Predecessor, Instigator, and Inheritor are implied. The leadership development program will be integrated into the leadership intervention. The basic principles of Girl Scouting are contained in the four program goals, the Girl Scout Promise and Law, and the traditions involved in the Girl Scout organization (GSUSA, 1995). *The Four Program Goals* of Girl Scouting are (a) developing to your full individual potential; (b) relating to others with increasing understanding, skill, and respect; (c) developing values to guide your actions and to provide the foundation for sound decision-making; (d) contributing to the improvement of society through the use of your abilities and leadership

References

Aguilar, F. J. (1967). *Scanning the business environment*. New York: MacMillan Company.

Butler, M. (2007). Latinas taking the lead. An unpublished proposed dissertation. Sam Houston State University.

Dornfield-Januzzi, J. (2006). *Adult perceptions of bullying by boys and girls in middle school*. Fordham University. DAI-A 67/03.

Eisenhardt, K. M. (1989). Building theories from case study research. *Academy of Management Review, 14*(4), 532-550.

Foster, V. (2006). *A qualitative investigation of the counseling experiences of college-aged women with a history of self*. The College of William and Mary. DAI-A 67/03.

Irby, B. J., & Brown, G. (1998). Exploratory sudy regarding the status of women's educational administrative support organizations. *Advancing Women in Leadership Journal*. Retrieved on September 15, 2006 from http://www.advancingwomen.com/awl/winter98/awlv2_irby6final.html.

Lee, T. W. (1999). *Using qualitative methods in organizational research*. Thousand Oaks, CA: Sage.

May, V. (1999). The Ideologue, the Pervert, and the Nurturer, or, Negotiating Student Perceptions in Teaching Introductory Women's Studies Courses In Winkler, B. S. & DiPalma, C. (Eds.). *Teaching Introduction to Women's Studies: Expectations and Strategies*. Westport, CT: Bergin & Garvey. Retrieved November 6, 2006, from Questia database: http://www.questia.com/PM.qst?a=o&d=27574317

Merriam, S. B. (1998). Qualitative research and case study applications in education. San Fransisco: Jossey-Bass Publishers.

Patton, M. Q. (1999). Enhancing the quality and credibility of qualitative analysis. *Health Services Research, 34*(5), 1189-1208.

Thibodeau, J. (1994). *Les facteurs de succès àl'exportation chez les PME manufacturières du Québec: une étude de cas multiples*. Unpublished master thesis, Université Laval, Québec.

Yin, R. K. (1993). *Applications of case study research*. Newbury Park, CA: Sage.

Yin, R. K. (1994). *Case study research: design and methods* (2nd ed). Thousand Oaks, CA: Sage.

Yin, R. K. (1997). The abridged version of case study research, design and methods. In L. Bickman & D. G. Rog (Eds), *Handbook of applied social research methods* (pp. 229-259). Thousand Oaks, CA: Sage.

TIP #5 GO THROUGH THE INTERNAL REVIEW BOARD (IRB) AND DEVELOP YOUR RESEARCH DESIGN

A prerequisite for conducting any research is obtaining consent to conduct the study. Sounds simple enough, but this process often involves several steps. In a university setting, obtaining this permission typically involves the Internal Review Board, commonly known as the IRB. The IRB is charged with protecting the rights of human subjects—in other words, ensuring that your study will cause no harm to your participants. The IRB also ensures that your study is ethical and just, meaning that you are not gathering data that are compromised or obtained through deceitful or inappropriate processes. Research in education is often fairly easy to get approved, simply

> *IRB stands for Internal Review Board. An IRB approval for any research project is necessary to maintain ethical practices within a study.*

because our research is often not experimental in nature, where one group receives a treatment and one group does not.

Step 1: Obtain Your *HPPERT Certificate*

Obtaining IRB approval for any research conducted under a federally funded institution (such as a university) now requires a Human Participant Protections Education for Research Teams (HPPERT) certificate. This certificate is awarded at the successful completion of a quiz regarding the rights of human subjects involved in research studies; this quiz is available electronically and free of charge through the National Cancer Institute's website at www.cancer.gov (2006):

> This free, web-based course presents information about the rights and welfare of human participants in research. The two-hour tutorial is designed for those involved in conducting research involving human participants. It satisfies the NIH human subjects training requirement for obtaining Federal Funds. You will have the option of printing a certificate of completion from your computer upon completing the course.

Step 2: Obtain Local IRB Approval

Whatever university you are attending, there are local policies and procedures regarding research with human subjects and the means for obtaining approval to conduct such research. In addition, most institutions will only grant permission for research in educational settings once you have received written permission at the local level (school campus or district) to conduct the study. For example, if you are planning to interview teachers on a highly successful campus, you will need a letter of permission from the school district in which that campus is located before the university will consider granting you permission to conduct the study.

The procedures and formality of the process for obtaining this local level of approval vary widely and are often dependent on factors such as the size of the school district. Some districts may have a formal application that you submit to receive permission; others may simply require that you ask the superintendent to sign a simple letter granting permission. Regardless, a letter of approval from the local group or individual must be obtained. This letter is then submitted as an attachment with your university human subjects approval form.

Participant Consent Form

Another required component of any research project is the participant consent form. This form is the letter that your actual participants' will sign, giving you consent to interview them and to use their responses in your study. This letter is critical, since your data are only valid and usable if you have this form signed for each participant.

When submitting your forms for IRB approval, only a sample consent form is needed. The actual signed forms will be part of your data and will be submitted to your professor at the conclusion of the study. You do not submit signed consent forms as part of your IRB application, because officially you do not have the university's approval to even conduct your study yet, much less approach participants about being involved in interviews. Additionally, you do not submit consent forms to a journal when submitting your work as a manuscript. A sample consent form appears below (Sam Houston State University, 2006a).

Template for Consent Forms

Instructions:

1. The following template provides the required elements that you will need to complete your consent form.

2. Do not remove anything in bold. Fill in the relevant information about your study below each bolded question or section. If you think one of the required elements is not applicable to your study, please provide a statement to that effect.

3. Instructions for each section are given in [*brackets and italic type*]. These italicized instructions should be deleted from the final document.

Informed Consent to Participate in Research

You (or your child) are being asked to participate in a research study. This form provides you with information about the study. The person handing you this form will also describe this study to you and answer all of your questions. Please read the information below and ask questions about anything you don't understand before deciding whether or not to take part in the study. Your participation is entirely voluntary and you can refuse to participate without penalty.

Title of Research Study:

Principal Investigator(s):

[*including faculty sponsor, university affiliation, and phone number(s)*]

Purpose of this study?

[*Include number and type of subjects and how they were identified or selected*]

What will you be asked to do if you take part in this research study?

[*Describe what participants will do. You may use bullets and briefly list the activities.*]

Time:

[*Approximate the length of time participants will be expected to devote to the study.*]

What are the possible discomforts or risks? [*There may be risks that are unknown at this time*]
If you wish to discuss the information above or any other risks you may experience, you may ask questions now or call the Principal Investigator listed on the front page of this form.

[*For studies that involve **psychological risk and/or emotional risk**, include the following*]

Many of the studies that are done by faculty/students do not involve physical risk, but rather the possibility of psychological and/or emotional risk from participation.

[*The principles that apply to studies that involve psychological risk or mental stress are similar to those that involve physical risk. Participants should be informed of the risk. They should be given the names and telephone numbers of agencies that may alleviate their mental concerns, such as a crisis hot line. If the principal investigator or the faculty sponsor of a student investigator is qualified to treat mental health problems, that person may be listed as a resource.*]

[*Studies on **sensitive topics**. Participants should be told that some of the questions are of a personal or sensitive nature and should be given examples of the topics or questions. They should also be told that they may skip a question if they do not wish to answer it. If questionnaires or interviews may generate reports of child physical or sexual abuse, the participant must be informed that the researcher is legally required to report this information to Child Protective Services. If the questionnaire or interview may generate reports that the participant plans to harm himself or herself or others, the participant must be told that the investigator is ethically required to report that information to the local police department. This information about the legal obligations to report abuse and threats of harm to oneself or others may be omitted if the responses are anonymous. In the event that the Privacy rule is more restrictive than the procedures described in the consent requirements, the more restrictive rule must be followed.*]

[*Studies using **deception**. Deception should be employed only when there are no viable alternative procedures. Where deception is a necessary part of an experiment, the PHSC will generally require that a preliminary consent be obtained, in which the investigator informs the subject that the experiment cannot be described fully in advance. After the experiment, the subject should be informed of the deception and its purpose. There may be rare instances in which no consent can be obtained or debriefing done. Deception requires that a PI get formal approval of a waiver of informed consent, due to the initial consent being used.*]

What are the possible benefits to you or to others?

[*If participants will not be paid, tell them that. It is possible that participants will receive no direct benefit from participation in this study. If so, tell them that.*]

What if you are injured during your participation in this study?

[*If this study involves some physical risk (e.g., some form of exercise), add a statement such as, "No treatment will be provided for research related injury, and no payment can be provided in the event of a medical problem."*]

If you do not want to take part in this study, what other options are available to you?

Participation in this study is entirely voluntary. You are free to refuse to be in the study, and your refusal will not influence current or future relationships with this university.

You are free to withdraw your consent and stop participation in this research study at any time without penalty.

If you have questions about your rights as a research participant, please contact **the Chair of the Protection of Human Subjects Committee (include phone number).**

How will your privacy and the confidentiality of your research records be protected?

[How long will they be kept and how will they be destroyed]

Authorized persons from this university and members of the Protection of Human Subjects Committee have the legal right to review your research records and will protect the confidentiality of those records to the extent permitted by law. Your research records will not be released without your consent unless required by law or a court order.

If the results of this research are published or presented at scientific meetings, your identity will not be disclosed.

*[For studies with **audio or video recordings**, participants must be told: (a) that the interviews or sessions will be audio or videotaped; (b) that the recordings will be coded so that no personally identifying information is visible on them; (c) that they will be kept in a secure place (e.g., a locked file cabinet in the investigator's office); (d) that they will be heard or viewed only for research purposes by the investigator and his or her associates; and (e) that they will be erased after they are transcribed or coded.]*

Name and signature of person who explained the purpose, the procedures, the benefits, and the risks that are involved in this research study:

_____

Signature and printed name of person obtained consent   Date

> **You have been informed about this study's purpose, procedures, possible benefits and risks, and you have received a copy of this form. You have been given the opportunity to ask questions before you sign, and you have been told that you can ask other questions at any time. Your signature on this page indicates that you understand what you are being asked to do, and you voluntarily agree to participate in this study. By signing this form, you are not waiving any of your legal rights.**
>
> _____
> Printed Name of Participant
>
> _____
> Signature of Participant   Date
>
> _____
> Signature of Principal Investigator   Date

Cover Letters

In some instances, a cover letter can replace a consent form. Usually this circumstance involves a low-risk survey research, where the cover letter includes a statement to the effect that "return of this survey indicates your informed consent." With these types of situations, your cover letter should be specific and should describe the purpose of the study along with a confidentiality agreement and a statement regarding how the data will be used. It should also include much of the assurances that the consent form contains, including the fact that respondents will not be penalized in any way for non-participation or for the content of their responses.

The biggest difference between consent forms and cover letters is that consent forms must be signed and returned; cover letters do not need to be signed or returned, because the return of the survey itself indicates that the participant is willing to be included.

University Human Subjects Approval Form

You must complete a Human Subjects Approval Form to be submitted to the university prior to actually conducting your research. As mentioned previously, you will need to look up your own school board (or whatever local agency you are using for your research) policy for Human Subjects protection and determine who will need to grant you permission to conduct the research within your district, campus, or institution of study. A letter from that institution granting you permission to conduct the study must be submitted with your Human Subjects Approval Form. Although these forms vary by institution, most request the same basic types of information. A sample classroom research form appears below (Sam Houston State University, 2006b). This is used for very low risk research studies. However, a formal Human Subjects Form must be completed on more moderate to high risk studies. For example, if you are a counseling doctoral student, and you wish to interview children about their involvement in pet therapy, then a full submission, not a classroom research form, would have to be submitted. Of course, prior to beginning your dissertation, you will need to complete a full application to conduct your research.

In general, these forms ask about the methodology of your study: who will your participants be, how will they be identified, how will they be contacted, what will you do with them? How will you collect your data? Will you do interviews, observations, focus groups, or surveys? Also, the IRB typically wants to know what your study will do with the data that you collect—will it be published, stored, or destroyed?

PROTECTION OF HUMAN SUBJECTS COMMITTEE

Classroom Research Form
All research projects must be submitted and approved
by the PHSC before the research may begin

Principal Investigator Name: Email
Research Associates Names:

☐ Graduate   ☐ Undergraduate
Instructor Name: Email
Course Name and Number: Section:
Research Title:
Description of Research:

Participants in Research

Number   Age Range   Gender ☐ Female   ☐ Male
Source of participants, selection criteria:

Methods:

☐ Survey/Questionnaire

☐ Direct Observation of Public Behavior

☐ Face-to-Face Interviews (not audio or video taped)

☐ Review of Existing Data

☐ Other: (Specify)

Proposed Dates for Research Project:

Level of Physical, Psychological, Emotional, or Legal Risk to Participants:
☐ None   ☐ Minimal   ☐ High

The following topics require a more thorough review by the PHSC and may require more time before a decision is made. Allow 2 to 4 weeks for expedited approval and longer for full committee review

The PHSC guide and application instructions can be accessed online.

Populations	**Topics**	**Settings**
Minors (under 18 yrs)	Alcohol/Drugs	Prisons
Prisoners	Depression/Suicide	Nursing Homes
Patients	Learning Disabilities	Hospitals
Physically or Mentally	Abortion/AIDS/HIV/Sex	Schools
Challenged Individuals	Sexually Transmitted Illness	Web Surveys /Chat
Pregnant Women	Body Image/Eating Disorders	Telephone
Elderly	Psychological Inventory	Outside Classroom
	Criminal Activity	

This list is not inclusive. If there are any questions regarding a population, topic, or setting requiring approval by the PHSC, contact the committee for the protection of human subjects.

This form must be typed or completed online. <u>Check for spelling and grammar.</u>
<u>Attach the following forms</u>

☐ Consent/Assent Forms

☐ HPPERT Certification

☐ Letter of Approval from Institution

☐ Survey/Interview Protocol

Student Signatures _____   Date _____
                          _____
                          _____
                          _____

Faculty/sponsor.

I have reviewed this application for accuracy and compliance with human subject protections. I approve the

☐ Purpose of the study

☐ Research design

☐ Consent/Assent form

☐ Method of subject selection

☐ Survey/interview protocol

☐ Plan for securing the data

I take responsibility for supervising the student(s) and monitoring the conduct of this project. I will report any adverse events to the PHSC.

Faculty Sponsor Signature _____   Date _____

Ethical Considerations

As an educational researcher, there are certain ethical guidelines that govern your research. First, you are bound by the notion to do no harm. Our research is intended to enlighten and inform, but never at the expense of physical or emotional hard to participants. While physical harm is rare in educational research, you should also take care to ensure that your research will cause no mental or emotional harm, such as embarrassment or ridicule for your participants. Second, you should maintain the utmost ethical standards in your research. Your reporting of procedures and findings should always be 100% honest, with no misrepresentation of your data, including misrepresentation by omission.

You also have ethical obligations to your participants in your research. If you have guaranteed them confidentiality as participants, then your research in no way should present any information that would make your subjects identifiable. Likewise, your reporting of what participants said should always be accurate and should be reported in the correct context. While all research requires high ethical standards, qualitative research above all others depends upon the integrity of the researcher.

Step 3: Decide on a Research Design

Research design refers to the blueprint or plan of study that a researcher uses. Because qualitative research involves inductive processes, the research design is less structured up front than in a traditional quantitative study. Several designs that are specific to qualitative research may be used, including case study, biography, ethnography, grounded theory, phenomenology, and historical discourse. Other more specific designs can also be used. Further information on qualitative research designs can be found in Bogdan and Biklen (2007), Creswell (2006), and Patton (2001).

Target Activities

Target 5: Learn about the IRB and the Research Design

A. Complete the sample Consent Form provided in the text for your study based on the sample provided in this chapter.

B. Find the Human Subjects Protection Forms and requirements for your university and complete the Human Subjects Protection form and make it specific for your study. Use the sample form provided or the actual forms required by your university.

C. Determine the type of research design that is appropriate for your study. Describe why this design is a good fit for your study. Does it allow you to adequately address your problem and purpose?

_____

_____

_____

_____

References

Bogdan, R.C., & Biklen, S.K. (2007). *Qualitative research for education: An introduction to theory and methods.* 5th ed. Needham Heights, MA: Allyn & Bacon.

Creswell, J.W. (2006). *Qualitative inquiry and research design: Choosing among five traditions.* Thousand Oaks, CA: Sage.

Patton, M.Q. (2001*). Qualitative research and evaluation methods.* Newbury Park, CA: Sage.

Sam Houston State University, Office of Research and Special Programs. (2006a). Consent letter. Retrieved August 18, 2006 from http://www.shsu.edu/~rgs

Sam Houston State University, Office of Research and Special Programs. (2006b). Classroom research form. Retrieved August 18, 2006 from http://www.shsu.edu/~rgs

TIP #6 DEVELOP YOUR CONTEXT, SAMPLE, AND INSTRUMENT

In Tip #6, we first present a very important concept that is central to qualitiative research, and that is context. After context, as next steps we discuss sampling techniques for obtaining participants. Finally, we present the development of instruments. All three of these sections should be placed in your paper under methodology.

Context Defined

What is meant by context of the study? As Bogdan and Biklen (2007) indicated,

Context takes the reader directly into the "place" of your study.

> ...action can best be understood when it is observed in the setting in which it occurs. These settings have to be understood in the historical life of the institutions of which they are a part. When the data with which they are concerned are prodcued by informants, as in the case of official records, qualitative researchers want to know where, how, and under what circumstances they came into being. Of what historical cirucumstances and movements are they a part? To divorce the act, word, or gesture from the context is for the qualitative researcher, to lose sight of significance. (pp. 4-5)

Context is usually the first side heading in your center heading section, methodology, in your paper.

Step 1: Describe Your Context

Readers of your study must be drawn into your study through your description of the context. This is the point at which you share with your readers the details of the "where" and "what" of your study.

It is not only important to have a good description of the context for the better understanding of the reader as he/she situates your findings in reality, there are several other reasons for describing the context in full. The context lends credibility to your study. For example, if your study is taking place on a campus, and you do not describe the context of the school in which your study takes place, you are leaving the reader to a guessing game, and your research is incomplete. If your study's data have emerged from students on an inner city campus, and your intent was to observe at-risk behavior in the hallways and the surrounding school grounds, it would be important to descibe the campus in detail, the demographics, the neighborhood, the structure of the day for the students, the hallways themselves with students and without students, and the bathrooms to depict the setting. What are the behaviors you will look for specifically? Describe those as well. While you may have some in mind, others will emerge from your observations. The data emerging from this setting or context can be understood then by the reader. The believability or the credibility is built partly through a rich description of the context.

Another reason for describing the context with such detail is that another student, like yourself, may wish to replicate your study in another locale. For example, if you have studied the at-risk behavior of students on an urban campus, someone else may wish to study similar behaviors in a suburban or rural setting or in another urban location.

There is yet even another reason for an in-depth description. This replication of studies in qualitative can be helpful, providing the research community with the ability to synthesize similar types of studies. However, in order to conduct a synthesis, an understanding of the context is critical. An accurate synthesis of similar research studies would need a cross-study analysis of the contexts of each study. Without an in-depth descriptoin of such, this type of cross-study synthesis would be near impossible and certainly weak.

Sample excerpts of a contexts of studies are shown in Figure 6.1. and 6.2.

Public, private and voluntary health sector organisations working in the field of HIV/AIDS in the city of Mumbai, India, were contacted for the study. The researcher knew about these organisations either because of her personal contacts with the organisations themselves or with people who knew them; or because she had heard about their work from other professionals or the media. Agreement of these organisations to assist the researcher was on a voluntary basis. Respondents from these organisations were chosen through purposive sampling (Morse, 1991). Caregivers with past or present experience of caring for male and/or female positive people, infected through the sexual and/or parenteral modes, who had moved beyond the asymptomatic stage and who had shared their serostatus with the caregiver were included in the study, regardless of whether the caregiver-care receiver relationship was based on blood or marital ties or whether the familial form was traditional or not (See Macklin, 1987, for a discussion on forms of family). Co-residence of the caregiver and care receiver was not a necessary criterion for participation. (Cruz, 2002, ¶ 7)

Figure 6.1. **Sample of context of study related to caregivers' experiences.**

This particular school was chosen because it provided sound information on the proficiency level of each participant. One distinguishing feature of the environment was the co-teaching system employed by the local government education bureau. The students received two hours of English classes taught by a native-speaking English teacher and a Chinese teacher (either a Chinese teacher with experience teaching English or a Chinese homeroom teacher). This city in the northern part of Taiwan was the very first to recruit native speakers of English to serve as EFL teachers for all of their public elementary schools in 2001. This project has therefore been regarded as a pioneering experiment in English education in the public school system in Taiwan.

Figure 6.2. **Sample of context of study related to English language learning.**

Another example of context may include both participants and context combined as Figure 6.3. demonstrates. Sometimes the context cannot be separated from the participants.

> The two schools in which this study was conducted were both designated high poverty, low performing schools with approximately 35% diversity (African-American, Asian, and Hispanic) with over half of the children in the school qualifying for free or reduced lunch. The schools had also been participants for three years in the federally funded Reading Excellence Act (REA) grant program. This grant targeted funds to teacher professional development in reading instruction, the establishment of home-school family literacy connections, and access to books and other reading and writing instructional materials to grade K-3 children, teachers, and their families in "high poverty, low performing" elementary schools.
>
> The children in these schools came from homes where one or more parents worked long hours, in some cases, two full eight hour shifts per day at low paying, minimum wage jobs. As a result of poverty, many of these children evidenced low oral language vocabularies generally and had fewer home literacy experiences. Across the two schools the predominant language spoken was English. However, as is the case in many southwestern communities, there is an increasing population of Spanish speaking parents and children. In the Spanish speaking homes, it was typical for the father to work long hours and for the mothers not to work outside the home at all or do so only part time. In the two schools participating in this study, approximately 20% of the parents and children spoke Spanish as their primary language.
>
> The study proceeded in three major phases. In the first phase of the study, after a year's participation in the Words-to-Go program, the parents, children's and teachers' perceptions of the program in four first-grade classrooms were assessed through distribution and analysis of an evaluation survey in late April of the first-grade year. Four first-grade teachers, fifty-four parents, and sixty-seven first-grade children responded to three separate evaluation surveys about the efficacy of the Words-to-Go program. In the second major phase of the study, several Words-to-Go focus group meetings were held at the school. The focus group meetings included randomly selected parents, first-grade children, the school principal, and all four participating first-grade teachers.
>
> In the third and final phase of the study, the four first grade classrooms involved in the Words-to-Go program were matched with four first-grade classrooms in another high poverty, low performing school that was also participating in the Reading Excellence Act grant. This resulted in eight first-grade classrooms for a final total of 144 first-grade children (n = 67 in the Words-to-Go program treatment group and n = 77 in the matched school where children received the same in-school phonics instructional program as well as participating in the same comprehensive family literacy program but did not participate in the Words-to-Go parent involvement portion of the program). The students' pretest and posttest scores in the two matched schools were used to compare the end-of-year first-grade student performance on a word reading task, a word writing (spelling) task, and a posttest only criterion referenced, end-of-level or end-of-year state reading test. (Ruetzal, et al., 2006, ¶ 17-20)

Figure 6.3. **Excerpt of qualitative research in which participants and context are interwoven.**

Step 2: **Reflect on Your Relationship to the Context**

As reported by Bogdan and Biklen (2007), researchers have been concerned with "charges that is it too easy for the prejudices and attitudes of the researcher to bias the data. ...the worry of subjectivity arises" (p. 37). They suggested that "The data must bear the weight of any interpretation, so the researcher must continually confront his or her own opinions and prejudices with the data. ...the researcher's primary goal is to add to knowledge, not to pass judgment on a setting" (pp. 37-38).

You must not be so concerned about being in control of your own personal perspectives you are paralyzed to move forward in your research. Simply acknowledge your perspective within the context of your study. Continue to consider it as you go into your setting and continue to reflect upon it as you analyze your data. Bogdan and Biklen stated, "Being a clean slate is neither possible nor desirable" (p. 38). The best thing to do is just be upfront about any perspective and past experiences you may have related to your topic. Figure 6.4 presents a sample of a researcher's perspective.

As a clinical psychologist in private practice for 10 years, I have a special interest in individual psychotherapy for adults and hypnotherapy, especially medical hypno-analysis. This approach enables me to help the patients in a short-term, dynamic, and creative way with many options from which to choose. I chose this holistic perspective by exploring and treating the origin of the *dis-ease* in the patient's subconscious mind in order to reach specific outcomes and facilitate health in his or her body, mind, and soul. Based on my practice background, I thought I could make a contribution in the area of self-esteem and hypnotherapy, in the discipline of psychology. Doing research in this area also gave me the opportunity to integrate different thoughts, knowledge, insights, and perspectives I gained over a period of approximately 10 years of working with psychotherapeutic patients with self-esteem issues. The research I did enabled me to obtain my doctorate in psychology in the process.

In this research project, I (as a therapist as well as a researcher) had a close therapeutic and professional relationship with the 11 research participants. Therefore, I could not be totally free of values or distant and be objective in my attitude towards them. This also applies to the nature of the qualitative research I did in this research project. Both my supervisors and I were deeply touched by the intensity and meaningfulness of the data we analyzed qualitatively, in accordance with the principles of the grounded theory. p. 187

Figure 6.4. **Researcher's perspective/bias sample**.

Sample

Since you are conducting qualitative research, you will most likely be relying on purposive sampling or selection of your participants. Specifically, that means that participants are selected based on their ability to provide their perspectives on a subject or they are within the context being studied. There are additional samples you can draw in qualitative research that we will share with you in this tip.

Step 2: **Determine Your Sample and Size of Sample**

Many of our students begin with the question, "How many participants do I need?" Of course, in quantitative designs, you may determine sample size by using power analysis and by reviewing other studies similar in nature to the one you are designing. However, in a purely qualitative study, we would not use a power analysis; however, we can go to previous studies related to our topic and capture the number of participants in each study on a table which may provide supporting evidence for the selection of a specific number of participants.

If you were interested in conducting a study of a specific phenomenon related to English language learners at the secondary level, you might conduct a review of literature using those keywords. Of course, you could be more specific and include the phenomenon being studied, but for our purposes, we reviewed some of the literature from 2003 to 2006 with the keywords of English language learners and adolescents. We purveyed the sample sizes in five studies that included qualitative designs. As indicated in Table 6.1, sample sizes ranged from one to 379. The answer to the question of "how many?" is "it depends." It actually depends on your purpose and the direction in which your study may take you. You will want to discuss the numbers with your professor for the course or your dissertation advisor.

Discuss the numbers for your sample with your professor.

63

Table 6.1
Sample Sizes within Studies on English Language Learning Students

Study Author	Date	Sampling Technique	Sample
Ajayi, L.J.	*2006*	*Total student Population, three middle schools*	*209*
Cartiera, M.	*2006*	*Convenience sample Connecticut public/private Institutions, teacher educators*	*26*
Rubinstein-Avila, E.	*2004*	*Selected sample within sample (original 227 students)*	*4 (1)*
Lan & Oxford	*2003*	*Total student population, Sixth grade students, One Taiwanese school*	*379*

Who or what your sample is determined by your purpose. Your sample may include individuals, cases, adults; children; archived data such as newsletters, school records, newspapers, photos, artwork, schoolwork; and/or documents collected in real time from participants.

Step 4: **Determine Your Technique(s) of Sampling**

As you already know, quantitative sampling depends on the power to generalize findings, but in qualitative research, it is not the generalization we are concerned with, rather it is a deeper understanding within a context that is the concern. Most qualitative researchers select purposive, or purposeful, sampling for their technique. In this technique participants, archived data, or documents are selected because they are representative of specific criterion the researcher is interested in studying. For example, if you are seeking to learn more about a specific teaching method, you would purposefully select teachers who have used the technique. You might want to stratify your sample into teachers who have used the method one year, two years, and more than two years, or you might want to stratify the sample into teachers who have had specific training on the method and those who have not. Perhaps you could develop an interview protocol for the teachers and an observation schedule with some videotaping.[1] Figure 6.5 provides a different purposive sampling example.

---

[1] Just a mention here is necessary related to the consent form: be certain to obtain their consent prior to the interviews and the observations. All of these procedures would have been approved prior to beginning your study with the IRB Committee within the university and the school district or agency.

Purposive sampling was employed to select the participants; this involved the establishment of criteria that identified participants who were rich in information relevant to the research question (Patton, 1990). Three criteria were used in the purposive sampling process: (i) players had to be currently playing rugby and to have had at least 10 years rugby playing experience, (ii) they had to have been involved in their current rugby club for at least two years, and (iii) they had to perceive rugby to be their most important sport. These criteria were designed to identify participants who had considerable experience in their sport, especially a childhood socialization in a rugby context. Finally, participants who rated rugby as their most important sport were selected as these players were more likely to have a clear understanding of their achievement goal orientations with respect to rugby. (Tod & Hodge, 2001, p. 307)

Figure 6.5. **Purposive sampling example**.

In Table 6.2, we present Patton's (2002) 16 types of purposeful sampling techniques from which you might choose along with our examples and recommendations for sample size. Although we provide this guideline for size, we are aware that this is truly hard to determine. As we say to our students, "Your sample size depends on your purpose, your topic, the issues of credibility, your time and resources." Lincoln and Guba (1985) would add that sampling is conducted "to the point of redundancy…. If the purpose is to maximize information, the sampling is terminated when no new information is forthcoming from new sampled units; thus *redundancy* is the primary criterion" (p. 202).

Table 6.2
Patton's (2002) Purposeful Sampling Techniques (pp. 230-242) with Our Added Examples and Suggested Numbers of Participants

Technique	Description
Extreme or Deviant Case Sampling	Selection of information-rich cases because they are unusual. (Example: Sample of exemplary elementary schools that also house an above 50% rate of low SES student population; Number: 4 to 65)
Intensity Sampling	Selection of information-rich cases that exhibit the studied phenomenon intensely, but not extremely. (Example: Sample of schools that have included parent involvement over a five-year period and have an established level of parent involvement on the campus; Number: 4 to 300)

Maximum Variation Sampling	Selection of a wide range of variation among participants on a central theme(s). (Example: Sample of rural, suburban, and urban campus principals in the north, south, east, and western portions of the state to determine shared patterns, as well as differences that emerge related to teacher quality; Number: 10 to 40 are commonly found in the literature; on occasion, you might find up to 200 in a sample using an open-ended questionnaire)
Homogeneous samples	Selection of a small, homogeneous sample. (Example: Female educational leaders who had rich experiences in high school as leaders in athletics; Number: 5 to 24)
Typical Case Sampling	Selection of the sample is based on the fact that it is the "norm" or "typical." (Example: Selection of a school that has an average or acceptable rating in achievement over the past three years; Number: 1 to 4)
Stratified Purposeful	Selection of samples within samples of particular subgroups (Example: Typical case sampling may be combined with maximum variation in this technique; for example, the selection of schools that represent a specific socioeconomic level with nested rural, urban, and suburban schools; Number: 10 to 20)
Critical Case Sampling	Select a critical case that will allow for logical, not technical, generalization and maximum application of information based on the logic that if it's true or if it happens within this one case, then it's likely to be true or happens in all other cases. (Example: Critical case of a 98% Hispanic, 75% Spanish-speaking homes and the potential for implementation of a one-way dual language program; Number: 1)

Snowball or Chain Sampling	Information-rich individuals or critical cases selected because they know a lot about a situation or are representative of a specific interest and are recommended by people who know quite a bit about the topic themselves. (Example: Snowball sample of professional Indian nationals who live in Texas who would have an opinion about the situation of counseling services in India; Number: 4 to 20)
Criterion Sampling	Selection of all cases that meet some criterion. (Example: All children who are seen in a university counseling clinic within a semester; if quality assurance standard it applied, the sample may be all children's cases whose diagnosis was able to be identified by students within a specified number of play therapy sessions and all that did not fit that standard would be studied; critical incidents could warrant a sample and as an example, the sample may be all children who were seen in a specific counseling clinic as a result of living near the Ground Zero during and after 9-11; Number: 2 to 30)
Theory-Based or Operational Construct	Selection of incidents, time periods, life experiences, or people based on their representation of a specified theoretical construct. (Example: Three women who demonstrated resiliency before, during, and after desegregation; A construct example would be when an individual works in schools with some specified criteria attempting to determine the construct of technology-rich teaching via constant comparative method (Strauss & Corbin, 1998); Numbers: 4 to 30).
Confirming or Disconfirming	Selection of cases that may elaborate and deepen initial analysis or that may be an exception to initial findings. (Example: 2 to 6)

Opportunistic or Emergent Sampling	Selection of sample within fieldwork as data emerges and opportunities arise. (Example: A first grade team of teachers and their classrooms are being used in the sample to study the impact of team planning on student learning, and while conducting the fieldwork of observation and interview, you observe other teachers in other grade levels who are working quite well as a team and this was observed as you had lunch daily during the time this grade level also had lunch. You may wish to take this opportunity to expand your observations and use this team to get a better understanding of cross-grade level differences or similarities. Numbers: Varies from two cases as provided in the example to 100s of individuals as opportunities arise during fieldwork)
Purposeful Random Sampling	Selection of a sample via a systematized and randomized procedure prior to the initiation of the study. This is not a representative sample of the population; therefore, generalizations cannot be drawn, but the sampling technique exemplifies randomization in a specific group and therefore assists with credibility. (Example: 500 parents have approved their and their child's participation in a large scale study related to an instruction intervention with parent support; being impossible to interview all 500 parents related to the intervention and success of their child, a random sample of 50 of the parents is drawn for a 20 minute interview each. Number: 10 to 60)
Politically Important Case Sampling	Selection of a politically sensitive site or unit of analysis. (Example: Border security related to illegal immigration may be studied in El Paso as it relates to education of children and the economy of the State. Number: 1 to 5)

Convenience Sampling	Selection of sample based on convenience (This is the least credible of all techniques as it is not purposeful nor is it strategic. Example: Because of time and money, a researcher decides to use the football team on his own campus as a case to study related to some specific athletic phenomenon. Number: 1 to 100)
Combination or Mixed Purposeful	Selection of sample based on a combination of the techniques listed herein. (Example: Politically Important Case Sampling may be used to select a specific case related to universities becoming accredited by a professional organization. During the course of the study, it may become apparent that an Emergent Sample is appropriate or perhaps even a Snowball Sample if the study warrants moving to other important case reviews. Number: Dependant upon the type of study in which the samples could range from two to over 100)

Note: The numbers are not a hard and fast rule. They are simply suggested based on commonly found samples in the literature.

Patton indicated limitations in sampling can cause problems in the study if there is insufficient breadth in sampling, incongruence revealed by changes over time, and a lack of depth in data collection (Patton, 2002).

Instrumentation

When we teach students how to write the methodology section of their research paper, there is a section within it on instrumentation. In our first few class meetings, we talk to our students about their "being the instrument." In fact, we show a short clip from the movie, Shanghai Noon, in which the main character is in a gunfight in the middle of the street, and he is saying to himself, "be the bullet." We equate that to "be the instrument." That is the basis of instrumentation in qualitative research.

 ## *Step 5*: **Decide Upon Your Instrument**

As a qualitative researcher, you will need to be keenly aware of yourself as the primary instrument through which all information is filtered. Through the positive interactions with respondents or with the environment, rich data are gathered related to the experiences and lives of those being studied. The researcher as instrument, does what an instrument in quantitative research primarily does. The researcher provides the purpose, communicates with the respondent, offers opportunities for the respondent to give relevant information, controls the flow of conversations, and the filter of evidence gathered. It is the researcher who interprets the data gathered and gives it meaning. All instruments used in qualitative research has as their base—the researcher as instrument. Because of this, it is important for the researcher to reflect upon his/her biases or perspectives as discussed earlier. There are basically two ways that most students are able to complete their project within the semester: (a) interviews (individual or focus groups), thus requiring an interview protocol, (b) survey or open-ended questionnaire, and/or (c) document analysis.

The Interview Protocol

In a semi-structured or structured interview process, you will need to develop an instrument with questions. This is called the interview protocol because it contains the format you will use to gather information from the respondent.

Confusion ensues sometimes with students related to whether the questions on the interview protocol are the research questions. They are not. If your study includes research questions, they will be related to the purpose of the study. Of course, the interview protocol questions will be too; however, these questions are the specific ones you will ask of the respondents and are not the research questions. For example, one of our students used this protocol during a semester:

1. How is counseling viewed in India?

2. After I explain to you the community counseling model, please share with me how you believe this model might be viewed by the following individuals:

    a. Priest
    b. Teacher
    c. Police officer
    d. Judge
    e. Parent
    f. Students
    g. Yourself if you were living in India again

3. How do you believe Americans view counseling differently from Indians?

4. Is there a religious connection to counseling? Why or why not?

5. If counseling services were set up in India, what do you think the steps would be to go about establishing such services?

The research question for her study was: "What implications might the implementation of counseling services have on the Indian community through the eyes of a community member?" Actually, you can see the difference between the research question and the actual interview protocol that was used.

We have several hints for the development of your protocol. They are:

1. Use questions that will allow for the most rich responses. Example: Share your changes in the district over the past year, and how has your leadership shaped change in the district?

2. Give more broad questions at first and then narrow the questions to get more to the point. Example: These are individual interview question examples from a student's study conducted on counselors as leaders—(a) How do you perceive your current role as a counselor?, (b) What do you do during the course of a day as a counselor?, (c) How does your administrator view your role?, (d) Do you consider yourself a leader on the campus and how?, and (e) Provide some examples of your leadership on the campus.

3. Validate the instrument. Just as in quantitative studies, the instruments developed by researchers are piloted, so too should the instruments in qualitative studies be piloted. We suggest that content validity and face validity are two types of validity that can be obtained. By content validity in the qualitative research, we mean the degree to which the instrument corresponds to the phenomenon, case, or topic being studied.

Content validity is demonstrated by making connections from the protocol to the concepts within the study itself. You may have a panel of experts to review the questions in the protocol and determine the degree of connectedness the protocol has to the content of the study. You would need to provide the panel with as much detailed information, including your theoretical framework, your purpose, your research questions, and your review of literature so that they could make an informed decision about the degree of connectedness.

Face validity is similar to content validity, but relates directly to the question content. Do the questions in the protocol measure what they are intended to measure? You will want to pilot the protocol with a couple of similar respondents or at least four members in a focus group like those who will be in your sample. Review their responses; are you getting what you feel is needed to answer your research questions? Are the question eliciting rich, thick descriptions from the respondents so that the research questions, themselves can be answered? You may have assistance in determining this as well via the same expert panel you used for establishing content validity or via a couple of other experts. You may determine that based on the pilot, the instrument needs altering.

4. The protocol questions may be probed with the respondent. For example, if a question is asked and the respondent(s) give(s) a short answer or an incomplete answer, you may wish to probe that question which is basically asking a follow-up question(s). You will need to make note of the probe in your fieldnotes on the protocol, and note that in the results as a deviation from the structured interview protocol. Of course, it will show up in the transcription that will be verbatim.

Survey

The open-ended survey or questionnaire is preferred in qualitative research because it provides more complex answers than closed form surveys. Open-ended surveys are developed similarly as in the above steps in the interview protocol. However, the survey is handled differently in terms of how to send it out to the individuals. You may determine that you want to use an online form vendor such as Formsite or Survey Monkey. There are several others so you will want to conduct a web search to find others. An example of a survey follows that is clear and simple, short questions that yield sufficient and rich discussion, a few closed questions, and points of reference are provided for the completer of the survey. The survey is long enough to gather important information on the topic; however, a follow-up interview may be necessary with some of the respondents for clarification purposes.

Counselor Questionnaire
(Use the back of this paper for your responses, if needed)

1. What grade levels are on your campus?
2. Are you a member of the Problem-Solving Team? If so, what position do you hold?
3. What is your understanding of the Problem-Solving Team process?
4. What is your understanding of Response-to-Interventions?
5. In what ways do you assist with the interventions designed by the Problem-Solving Team?
6. How do you verify that the interventions have been executed by teachers or specialist?
7. What is your perception or understanding of "No Child Left Behind" in terms of "students at risk"?
8. What role do you believe school counselors play in the Individuals with Disabilities
   Education Act (IDEA) of 2004 in terms of "Response-to-Interventions?
9. What do you do on your campus to assist at-risk students?
10. How many years of counseling experience do you currently have?

Figure 6.6. **Example of survey with closed and open-ended questions.**

The survey or the interview protocol are the most logical instruments to use during a semester. There are times when documents can be analyzed that might lend support to your study, but with limited time available during a semester to complete a full research study, the survey or interview techniques for instruments are advised.

Target Activities

Target 6.   Context, Sample, and Instrument

A. Design your context. Be certain that you are explicit and bring the reader right into the location of your study.

_____
_____
_____
_____
_____
_____

B. Determine which sampling technique you will use for your study. Write the sample section of your study. Be specific as to how and why you are sampling what and whom.

_____
_____
_____
_____
_____

C. Design your instrument. Be certain to include how you developed your instrument and the procedure for your instrument for establishing content and face validity. Also, write about how you will follow up with respondents who do not submit a survey.

_____
_____
_____
_____

D. Critique the following excerpts of context, sample, and instrument. Use the steps and tips presented in this chapter to complete your critique.

Critique 1. Context and Sample (this example combined the two)

Participants and Setting

Ten intercultural couples were chosen for this study. For the purpose of this study, the participants were required to have been married for a minimum of five years and are parents of at least one child. The couples were known to us and were supportive of the study, and thus willingly provided information to us. The intercultural couples were required to complete a demographic survey prior to the audio-taped interview. The demographic survey was emailed to the couples using the Survey Monkey Internet collection system. All couples completed the survey online and results were forwarded to us via email. After completion of the demographic survey, we completed scheduled interviews with the couples. Individual rights to privacy and confidentiality were maintained during research process and thus names of the couples involved in the research study will not be disclosed. (Unpublished research paper, Doctoral student, Sarah Brand- used with permission)

Critique 2. Sample and Instrument (the sample and instrument were combined in this example)

Participants

A sample of 254 instructors of multicultural courses at CACREP accredited counseling programs was drawn. The method utilized to compile the sample came via an exhaustive website search of the current CACREP accredited programs listed on the CACREP website. Instructors invited to participate in the open-ended survey were those either, at the time of the survey distribution, currently teaching a multicultural course or were previously listed as having taught a multicultural course to masters level counseling students. The selected instructors were contacted via e-mail to participate in the survey with open-ended responses.

After the initial survey was sent, 46 e-mail responses were received from respective e-mail servers with delivery error messages (18%). There were four direct responses from contacted instructors asking to be taken off of the survey delivery list (.02%). Of those who ultimately received the survey, 34 instructors provided open-ended responses (16.7%).

The mean age of the survey responders was 47.5 years, with the range spanning 27 years of age to 75 years of age. There were 26 female respondents (76.5%) and eight male respondents (23.5%). The racial make-up of those who responded to the survey consisted of 19 Caucasian/White (55.9%), five African American/Black (14.7%), four Asian/Asian American (11.7%), one American Indian (3%), one Mexican American (3%) and four Biracial Identification (11.7%). The Biracial Identification group, as self described, consisted of one "Biracial Asian-American," one "Mixed-European & native (Indian)," one "White, some American Indian," and one "Euro/Caucasian & Latina." There were nine United States regional locations represented by respondents: six Eastern U.S. (18.2%), six Southeastern U.S. (18.2%), six Midwestern U.S. (18.2%), five Southwestern U.S. (15.2%), three Middle U.S. (9%), two Southern U.S. (6%), two Northeast U.S. (6%), two Northwest U.S. (6%), and one Western U.S. (3%).

The open-ended question of religious preference spawned an array of responses. Nine respondents stated none (28.1%), five Protestant (15.6%), four Christian (12.5%), three Baptist (9.4%), two Catholic (6.3%), two Unitarian (6.3%), and one of each of the following: Methodist (3%), Presbyterian (3.1%), Buddhist (3.1%), Jewish (3.1%), Eclectic (3.1%), Agnostic (3.1%), and Atheist (3.1%). When asked to identify sexual orientation, 28 respondents replied as being heterosexual (82.3%), four stated being bisexual (11.7%), and two answered as being homosexual (6%). With regards to the identified academic department each respondent affiliated themselves with, 29 were in the department of counselor education (85%), two in the psychology department (6%), one in the human services department (3%), one in the student affairs department (3%), and one in the education department (3%). (Unpublished research paper, Michael Maxwell, used with permission)

Critique 3. Participants

Participants

A stratified purposeful sample of participants was gathered. Stratified purposeful sampling "includes several cases at defined points of variation . . . with respect to the phenomena being studied" (Gall, Gall, & Borg, 2003, p. 179). The different points of variation that were considered included low-risk, borderline, and high-risk couples (determined by their scores on the Dyadic Adjustment Scale). Additional points of variation included ethnicity of the participants.

Participants included at least four heterosexual couples, representing four different ethnicities. The couples were recruited using flyers describing the research study, which were posted in public domains as well as distributed by other counselors. The flyers included information about the study and its importance, what types of participants were needed, the importance of participating, when and where to obtain further information about participating, and incentives for participating. Persons interested in taking part in the study contacted the researcher by telephone to schedule a day, time, and location to meet for the interview process, or to ask questions related to participation in the study.

Critique 4. Instrumentation

Instrumentation

The data collection will consist of two portions: demographic information and participant responses. Demographic informational questions will include gender, race, level of experience, and important cultural perspectives relevant to the study. RPT-S perception questions will be created to gain knowledge about the perspectives of practitioners in regards to key skill components. The questions will only focus on these areas and will not ask for any identifying information on the participants. Any surfacing identifying information included in the interviews or questionnaires will be coded to protect the participants' identity an perceived role within the field of play therapy.

Procedural Methods

A sample of 15 RPT-S participants will be obtained from the Association for Play Therapy, Inc. and Sam Houston Association for Play Therapy. Participants will be involved in a structured interview or open-ended questionnaire. The determining factor for modality of obtaining the research information will be dictated by the location of the participant. Local participants (living within 60 miles of the researchers) will be asked to participate in the structured interview, while distant participants (living more than 60 miles from the researchers) will be asked to complete an online questionnaire.

Participants will be given a copy of an informed consent. The contents will be verbalized with each participant. An explanation of the informed consent process will include an explanation that the participant may choose to exit the study at any time with no penalty or obligation, and each individual will be advised that there is no compensation for involvement in the study.

Each participant's information will be processed in accordance with the way in which the data was obtained. Interviewed participant information will be coded to protect the identity of the participant. Interviews will be video taped and transcribed by a research assistant. All data will be kept in a locked file cabinet in the principal investigator's office. All coded data will be destroyed upon completion of the study.

Those participants involved in the questionnaire distribution will be electronically mailed an invitation to visit the questionnaire website. The electronically mailed document will include the informed consent and a cover letter. These documents will explain the purpose of the study, benefits of the study to the field of counseling, and possible risks related to the study. Participants will then be asked to visit a web-link attached in the electronic mail containing the questionnaire document.

Individuals participating in the direct interview will be invited to participate through an electronically mailed document and asked to respond to the document if he or she is interested in participating. The researchers will correspond with these participants to coordinate face-to-face interviews. (Unpublished research paper, Sara Kinsworthy, used with permission)

References

Ajayi, L. J. (2006). Multiple voices, multiple realities: Self-defined images of self among adolescent Hispanic English language learners. Education 126 (3), pp. 468-480.

Bogdan, R.C., & Biklen, S.K. (2007). *Qualitative research for education*. Boston, MA: Pearson Education, Inc.

D'Cruz, P. (2002). *Caregivers' experiences of informal support in the context of HIV/AIDS*. The Qualitative Report, *7(3). Retrieved on October 3, 2006 from http://www.nova.edu/ssss/QR/QR7-3/dcruz.html.*

Fawson, P.C., & Smith, J.A. (2006). Words to go! Evaluating a first-grade parent involvement program for "making" words at home. Reading Research and Instruction, 45 (20), pp. 119-159.

Lan, R., & Oxford, R.L. (2003). Language learning strategy profiles of elementary school students in Taiwan. *IRAL*, 41(4), pp. 339-379.

Patton, M. Q. (2002). *Qualitative evaluation and research methods* (3rd ed.). Newbury Park, CA: Sage Publications.

Reutzel, D.R., Cartiera, M.R. (2006). Addressing the literacy underachievement of adolescent English language learners: A call for teacher preparation and proficiency reform. The New England Reading Association Journal, 42 (1), pp. 26-32.

Rubinstein-Ávila, E. (2004). Conversing with Miquel: An adolescent English language learner struggling with later literacy development. *Journal of Adolescent & Adult Literacy 47(*4), pp. 290-301.

Tod, D., & Hodge, K. (2001). Moral Reasoning and Achievement Motivation in Sport: A Qualitative Inquiry. *Journal of Sport Behavior, 24*(3), 307. Retrieved November 19, 2006, from Questia database: http://www.questia.com/PM.qst?a=o&d=5002409887

Van Zyl, J., Conjé, E.M., & Payze, C. (2006). Low self-esteem of psychotherapy patients: A qualitative inquiry. *The Qualitative Report* 11 (1) pp. 182-208. Retrieved on November 3, 2006 from http://www.nova.edu/ssss/QR/QR11-1/vanzyl.pdf .

INCREASE THE RELIABILITY AND VALIDITY OF YOUR STUDY

Tip #7 is very important for qualitative research since it actually deals with how credible the entire study is perceived to be. Bodgan and Biklen (2007) stated that "In qualitative studies, researchers are concerned with the accruacy and comprehensiveness of their data and what actually occurs in the setting under stuy, rather than the literal consistency across different observation" (p. 40). In Tip #7, we share information related to making your study more reliable and valid, thus lending credibility to the work you will have done by the end of the semester. We say that credibility is everything in every way for the qualitative researcher.

Credibility: Everything in Every Way

Qualitatative research often is said to be "soft" science, "soft" research, yet from qualitative research techniques have come the law of gravity (use of critical case sampling and observation), "great" examples of company leadership (use of criterion sampling with 28 companies, Collins, 2001), Piaget's developmental stages (use of convenience sampling, observation, and fieldnotes), Freud's field of psychoanalysis (use of less than 10 clients, observation, and fieldnotes), and the field of scientific management (a single case study design based on observation, Taylor, 1911). Qualitative research is powerful and has led to much of what we believe and do in the world of business, education, psychology, counseling, and in life, in general. However, specificity in what the individuals named did was paramount to the credibility of their work. We share now with you how to make your study credible in every way possible.

Step 1: Use Guba's Model of Trustworthiness

One way in which you can improve the reliabilty and validity of your study if via the use of Guba's (1981) identification of four components of trustworthiness: (a) truth value, (b) applicability, (c) consistency, and (d) neutrality.

Truth Value

Here is your question for truth value: Have you established confidence the truth of your findings for the respondents and the context of the study? Lincoln and Guba (1985) actually used the term, credibility, when discussing this component and indicated that there is the assumption that a single tangile reality can be measured. Futhermore, they indicated that multiple realities can be represented as well. Truth value can be tested by testing findings against various groups from which the data are drawn. Another way to test it is to have someone who is a knowledgeable of the topic to review the data. A final way to test it is ensure that the descriptions from the respondents are so explicit that anyone reading the material who is familiar with the context would understand the realities from their own experiences in similar contexts.

Krefting (1991) provided the following ways to establish truth value. She first suggested prolonged and varied field experiences and noted that Lincoln and Guba (1985) termed that prolonged engagement. This, according to Krefting, "allows the researcher to check perspectives and allows the informatns to become accustomed to the researcher" (p. 215). She also suggested time sampling, reflexivity, triangulation, member checking, peer examination, interview technique, establishing authority of the researcher, structural cohorence, and referential adequacy.

Table 7.1.
Criteria and Brief Explanation of Kreftings (1991) Strategies for Establishing
Trustworthiness in Truth Value

Truth Value Strategy	Explanation
Prolonged Engagement	Time spent to engage the informants
Time Sampling	Dependant on design, explain specifically
Reflexivity	Reflect on your influence in the study and provide your own perceptions when appropriate
Triangulation	Cross checking of data, sources, and interpretation
Member Checking	Testing the data with the informants
Peer Examination	Discussion of data with experienced colleagues
Interview Techniques	A check on internal consistency in the interview where the same topic is discussed consistently within the interview
Establishing Authority of the Researcher	Degree of familiarity with the topic, knowledge base, and good investigative skills
Structural Coherence	Data and interpretations are consistent

Applicability

Here is your question for applicability: Can the findings be applied to other contexts or other groups or individuals—is the information applicable to others?
Of course, in quantitative research, we would liken this to generalizability, but for qualitative research, generalizability is not particularly relevant since we are usually attempting to seek a deeper understanding of unique lived experiences or phenonmena for example. However, Guba talked about qualitative research being applicable related to fittingness or transferability. He indicated that the findings could potentially "fit" into other contexts that are similar and suggested that transferability is beholden to the reader to transfer the information to other contexts for themselves. Make certain you have again described with great detail the findings and the context of your study so that any applicability questions could be resolved quickly.

Krefting (1991) provided the following ways to establish applicability. According to Krefting, applicability may not even be an issue if the researcher's philosophical stance is that in qualitative research one is not seeking to genderalize or transfer. However, even though there is situational uniqueness, she suggested the following ways to establish trustworthiness under applicability: nominated smaple, comparison of smaple to demographic data, time sample, and dense description. Table 7.2 presents this information with a brief explanation of each.

Table 7.2.
Criteria and Brief Explanation of Kreftings (1991) Strategies for Establishing Trustworthiness in Applicability

Applicability Strategy	Explanation
Nominated Sample	Panel of judges nominates the informants who are knowledgeable of the subject/topic
Comparison of Sample to Demographic	Compare the sample to the demographic information; add to the sample if needed as demographics become more clear through the fieldwork
Time Sampling	Sample is selected and come into the study at different points based on various criteria, in particular to transferability, it would be based on demographics
Dense Description	Intense desciptions of the informants and the context are important for the readers so that they may determine applicability. Dense description in the results section is also important.

Consistency

Here the question for your study becomes—Would you find similar findings if your replicated your study with the same sample or in a similar context? Guba indicated that consistency can be defined as dependability. Dependability of the data with the same participants or in a similar context must also consider variability. Guba suggested that vaiablitiy is attributed to sources that can be explained by the researcher. In this case, nothing can be left to scrutiny. Your insight into the variablitiy in sources, including the range of experiences of the respondents, as a researcher, is critical for consistency and the ability to appy findings across similar studies. Your detailed explanation of your own insights is important for a reader to be able to determine consistency from one study to another or one phase of the study to another. Krefting shared criteria for establishing trustworthiness related to constency and we share a brief explanation based on those criteria in Table 7.3.

Table 7.3.
Criteria and Brief Explanation of Kreftings (1991) Strategies for Establishing Trustworthiness in Consistency

Consistency Strategy	Explanation
Dependability Audit	A dense description of all components of methodology so that another researcher can utilize it to replicate the study
Stepwise Replication	The data are split; two researchers work independently with the data then compare results. Researchers are in continuous conversation.
Time Sampling	Sample is selected and come into the study at different points based on various criteria, in particular to transferability, it would be based on demographics
Dense Description	Intense desciptions of the informants and the context are important for the readers so that they may determine applicability. Dense description in the results section is also important.
Triangulation	Cross checking of data, sources, and interpretation
Peer Examination	Discussion of data with experienced colleagues
Code-Recode Procedure	After coding a set of data, the researcher waits two weeks and returns to recode the same set of data then compare results

Neutrality

The question we ask here is: Is the reporting of the data biased in any way by the research or research procedures? Of course, in this component, the researcher is not neutral due to the contact with the context and/or the participants. However, the data should be neutral coming directly from the respondents or actual observations from the fieldnotes or from documents gathered. The researcher must be able to confirm the neutrality of the data and the research procedures. Guba (1981) called this confirmability of the data. This is again accomplished by specificity in the writing of the research report. Krefting named specific strategies to establish trustworthiness in the area of confirmability. Those are listed in Table 7.4. We have added a brief explanation of each based on her work.

Table 7.4.
Criteria and Brief Explanation of Kreftings (1991) Strategies for Establishing Trustworthiness in Neutrality or Confirmability

Confirmability Strategy	Explanation
Confimability Audit	Another researcher attempts to follow the research design, method, progression of the project, and determines why the other researcher did what he/she did—all components of the study are audited.
Triangulation	Cross checking of data, sources, and interpretation
Reflexivity	Reflect on your influence in the study and provide your own perceptions when appropriate

Step 1: Use Johnson's Strategies Related to Qualitative Research Validity

Johnson (1977) wrote about three types of validity in qualitative research. We believe it is advanatageous for you to consider this as you establish your study's reliability and validity. The five types of validity are: (a) descriptive validity, (b) interpretive validity, (c) theoretical validity, (d) internal validity, and (e) external validity.

Descriptive Validity

This type validity refers to the "the factual accuracy of the account as reported by the researchers" (Johnson, 1977, p. 283). A strategy that is useful to assist with description, the foundation of qualitative research, is investigator triangulation. In this strategy several researchers are used in collecting, analyzing, and interpreting the data.

Interpretive Validity

This type validity, according to Johnson, "requires developing a window into the minds of the people being studied" (p. 284). Basically, it refers to the accuracy with which the researcher interprets what the participants have attempted to share or portray. There are several strategies that might assist you in establishing interpretive validity of your study.

1.   Participant feedback, or member checking, simply put, is asking your participants if what you have taken as data and/or interpreted is accurate with what they thought they said or meant.

2.   Low inference descriptors is another strategy that you can use when you are writing your paper. In this case, you will report supporting documentation for a theme or category that emerges from the data. The supporting documentation will be in the form of words of the respondent(s), or verbatim quotes from the respondent.

Theoretical Validity

Theoretical validity is the "degree that a theoretical explanation developed from a research study fits the data and, therefore, is credible and defensible" (Johnson, 864). There are several beneficial strategies for accomplishing this type validity.

1.   Theory triangulation may be a beneficial strategy. This means that you would take your topic or phenonmenon being studied and explain that by differing theories.

2.   You may use extended fieldwork where you are in the field studying your research participants for a sufficient amount of time. This will provide you with the extensive data needed to build accurate patterns and determine relationships.

3.   Negative case sampling will assist you in finding cases that do not confirm your theoretical framework you are using.

4.   Peer review may be helpful in that you can discuss your findings with colleagues and deterine if you need additional data, particularly as the findings relate to underlying theory.

Internal Validity

This is the fourth kind of validity that "refers to the degree to which a researcher is justified in concluding that an observed relationship is causal" (Johnson, p. 864). Johnson suggests several strategies for internal validity.

1.   Researcher as detective is characterized when you search "forr evidence about causes and effects. The researcher develops an understanding of the data through careful considertation of potential causes and effects and by sytematically eliminating "rival" explanations or hypothese until the final 'case' is made 'beyond a reasonable doubt.' The 'detective' can utilize any of the strategies listed here (Johnson, p. 863).

2.   Methods triangulation can also be used under internal validity. Here you would use more than one type of methodology in your study. For example, you may use survey, interview, observation, field observation, etc.

3.   Data triangulation uses multiple data sources. For example you may use multiple interviews, observations, time periods, individuals, document types, or places.

External Validity

This type validity is critical to be able to generalize your findings. As indicated earlier generalizability is not a particular concern with qualitative research. However, you may be able to generalize across similar locations, individuals, groups, or institutions. You may will, as stated earlier, need to provide detailed information about your respondents in terms of numbers, culture, location, how they were determined to come into your study, context, your perspective and relationship to the respondents/participants, methods, data collection procedures, and analysis methods. Providing the reader this information will give them specific information needed to determine if the study is generalizable to another setting or if another researcher wishes to replicate the study.

You may use replication logic where you would determine how many times a specific finding has occurred in differing studies that have been basically replicated. You may even replicate your own study in differing settings.

You will need to determine which type of validity and reliability strategies you will use to assist in maintaining the integrity and credibility of your study. Following is an example of a section of a paper that relates validity and reliability of the study.

Credibility

The present qualitative research can be judged from the view point of credibility, transferability, dependability, and confirmability of this study. Credibility is based on the validity and reliability of the instruments or instruments used and the internal validity of the study. The reliability and validity of this qualitative research is fundamental to its utility. Credibility is supported by prolonged engagement, persistent observation, and appropriate selection of respondents. First, the study was performed over eight months period of time. A thorough observation and in-depth interview from the right person also ensure the dependability of the results. Hopefully, the findings are based on the analysis of reliable and valid qualitative information obtained from a few appropriately selected professionals, who are well acquainted with the subject and objective of the study on undocumented migration, and hence, results can be trusted to represent the real world situation. This study is not so concerned with the generalizability of the results; it has tried to achieve in-depth holistic understanding of the process and underlying causes of illegal migration across Indo-Bangladesh border.

Among the three non-probability sampling i.e., convenience sampling, quota sampling, and purposive sampling, this purposive sampling (Merriam, 1988; Patton, 1990) is the sampling approach mostly used by qualitative researchers with the intention to improve representativeness of the sample by subjective selection.

Though triangulation (Lincon & Guba, 1985; Bogdan & Biklen, 2007) in true sense of the term was not possible, but most of the results of the study converge to the information obtained from existing literature, newspaper, and magazine. Hence, confirmability is justified. Multiple listening of audio tape and multiple transcriptions from audio tape has been utilized to justify the validity of the results. Besides extensive quotations from field notes have been used to ensure validity of the results.

From a qualitative perspective, transferability is primarily the responsibility of the one doing the generalizing. I have enhanced transferability by doing a thorough description of the research context and the assumptions that were central to the research. (Datta, 2004, p. 343)

Figure 7.1. *Example of credibility in published study.*

Target Activities

 Target 7.   Determine How You Will Establish Credibility in Your Study

A.   Review a qualitative research study that has been published. Find how that individual addressed reliability and validity. Share this with a classmate.

Which did you review?

_____

How did it address reliability and validity of the study?

_____
_____
_____

B.   Which strategy might be most beneficial to your study and why?

_____
_____
_____

C.   Practice writing a deep description on a restaurant you visit this evening (setting, people, atmosphere, what was said to you by the staff from the moment you go in and until you leave).

_____
_____
_____
_____
_____
_____
_____
_____
_____
_____
_____
_____

_____
_____
_____
_____
_____
_____
_____
_____
_____
_____

D. Go with a friend to the restaurant. Be reflexive about your conversation. Write about your surface conversation, under the surface conversation, themes, your own thoughts about how the conversation went.

_____
_____
_____
_____
_____
_____
_____
_____
_____
_____

E. Write this section, Reliability and Validity of the Study, for your own research study.

_____
_____
_____
_____
_____
_____
_____
_____
_____
_____

References

Bogdan, R.C., & Biklen, S.K. (2007). *Qualitative research for education*. Boston, MA: Pearson Education, Inc.

Collins, J.C. (2001). *Good to great.* New York: Harper Collins.

Datta, P. (2004). Push-pull factors of undocumented migration from Bangladesh to West Bengal: A perception study. *The Qualitative Report 9* (2), 335-358.

Krefting, L. (1991). Rigor in qualitative research: The assessment of trustworthiness. *The American Journal of Occupational Therapy, 45,* 214-222.

TIP #8 COLLECT YOUR DATA

As in any study, collecting data is a critical component to the study's overall success. Your methods for data collection will determine whether or not you obtain useful data that produce meaningful results, or whether your data are shallow and surface level, with little or no practical use. Remember that qualitative studies are usually much smaller in scope than quantitative studies, but what they lack in breadth, they make up for in depth. Thus, your means of data collection and the data they produce are critical to your study and should be carefully considered.

> *Qualitative studies are usually much smaller in scope than quantitative studies, but what they lack in breadth, they make up for in depth.*

Step 1: **Understand the Types of Data**

Five types of data may typically be used in a qualitative study. These include interviews, observations, documents, focus groups, and surveys. Each type has strengths and weaknesses, and each can be considered appropriate or not for certain qualitative studies. As a researcher, you should evaluate the appropriateness of each type of data for your study. Appropriateness can include the type of data that can be generated, your access to such data, and the fit each type of data has with your problem and purpose.

Observations

Observations can be completed in two ways: participant or non-participant. Participant observations occur when the researcher is actually a part of the group being observed. Non-participant observations occur when the researcher is an "outsider," or not part of the actual group.

One thing to consider with observations is the Hawthorne effect, which suggests that behavior is altered simply because people are aware that they are being observed. As an observer, you would need to be sure that your presence is as least disruptive as possible. You should also be aware of any signs that indicate that your presence is altering the participants' natural behavior.

Documents

Documents can vary from the very personal to legal records that can be found on almost all people. Personal documents might include such items as diaries, letters, or other self-reported ideas written by an individual. They normally will detail personal reflections or feelings that a person has, which can provide valuable insight into that person's perceptions. Other types of documents might be organizational in nature; these can be internal documents, such as those shared within a department, or external documents, which are those things that an organization puts out for public consumption. Organizational documents might include employee memos, flyers, or salary records.

Electronic documents, which could include emails, blogs, or text messages, are a new form of document that should also be considered. Public records and personnel files can also be sources of important documents that provide key factual information about a person. These items could include grades, attendance, disciplinary records, employment history, letters of commendation (or reprimand), and other such communications. Public government documents such as marriage licenses, birth certificates, or death certificates could also be used in a study, as could documents such as medical records, court documents, or news media files.

A final source of documents is that developed through popular culture; this could include videos, movies and films, music, magazines, television shows, or advertisements. A person's interest or involvement with any of these media could reveal important insight into the person's likes, dislikes, or personality. While documents alone are rarely sufficient to conduct a qualitative study, they are excellent sources of support data for other things such as interviews and observations.

Surveys

Surveys are typically considered to be a tool for gathering quantitative data. Still, they can be useful in qualitative studies when they include open-ended questions where participants record their thoughts or perceptions on a given topic. The downside to using a survey to collect qualitative research is obvious. With a survey, you lack the opportunity to probe deeper into participants' responses. With a short answer or off-task answer, you are unable to ask for clarification or further detail. You are also unable to clarify yourself to the participants—if your questions are unclear, you have no way to explain what you mean to those persons completing the surveys. You also have no way to use any data other than what is written—there are no non-verbal cues, no body language, no facial expressions, no tone of voice, or any other contextual elements that might add to the richness of your data and findings. Thus, use caution in collecting qualitative data by surveys alone.

One further note of caution: people tend to elaborate more when they are speaking than when they are writing. In addition, writing responses takes more time and effort on the part of the participant than would a verbal response. So, your chances of getting the depth of responses with a survey are quite lower than with an interview or focus group setting.

Consider the importance of the following items in developing qualitative surveys. For each item, describe its importance in a qualitative context and what strategies you would use to ensure that this area of the survey was adequate:

Communicating your problem:

_____

_____

Giving clear instructions to participants

_____

_____

Making sure your questions are clear

_____

_____

Ensuring your questions will provide adequate data

_____

_____

Interviews

Interviews quite simply involve a question/answer process between the interview and one participant. Structured interviews, in which there is a purposeful set of pre-developed questions, are typically effective in qualitative studies, particularly with novice researchers. When developing interview questions, be sure that they align with the problem and purpose of your research study. Great questions are not so great if they do not relate to your purpose and fail to produce useful data. Questions should be open-ended and allow for maximum opportunities for participants to respond. Each question should ask only one thing, so that each important concept is addressed individually. Researchers should avoid leading questions that might convince or suggest to a participant that you are looking for a particular type of response. Interviewers must be prepared; you should avoid bias and always show the utmost respect for your respondents.

Whenever possible, tape record your interviews so that you can provide exact transcriptions of what was said. Interviews are a powerful tool that usually offer the best insight into a participant's thoughts, feelings, and perceptions about a particular topic. One good thing about an interview is that it allows for more than just verbal responses. In addition to the responses, you can observe body language, facial expressions, tone of voice, and other non-verbal cues. Let the purpose guide the interview process.

Focus Group

In essence, a focus group could be considered a group interview. When interviews are not possible, a focus group provides a quicker alternative to achieving personal responses. Typically a focus group involves 7-10 persons, plus a facilitator who may or may not be the researcher. Focus groups allow for multiple perspectives and allow participants to share ideas with one another. However, a strong personality could dominate a focus group and change or manipulate the ideas of others. Sometimes participants might be embarrassed to share their honest ideas in front of others, or they may be intimated to speak in front of more dominant personalities. You as the researcher should ensure that all members of the focus group are on task and feel safe and secure in what they say. Emphasize that there are no right or wrong answers, and that not everyone has to agree with one another. You should also ensure that the group remains respectful of all individuals and that everyone has an opportunity to be heard.

Step 2: **Address Your Bias**

In a qualitative study, you as the researcher are the instrument, since you are the tool by which data are gathered. Thus, you need to describe the instrument – your biases, assumptions, expectations, and history. Any number of factors can influence you as you collect data for your qualitative study. All of these areas of influence are sources of potential bias. Although it has a negative connotation, bias is not a bad thing – it does not mean that you are a good or bad person, or that you are not an objective researcher. It means that you are human. For example, your gender, ethnicity, religion, political affiliation, education level, income level, and occupation all impact the way in which you view things. They impact your decisions, your viewpoints, and your daily actions. Your experiences impact these things as well – they are all part of who you are and influence the lens through which you view the rest of the world.

It is not possible to eliminate all sources of bias as you conduct your qualitative study. What is necessary is to identify those areas of potential bias that could impact the study and its findings. For example, if you are studying bilingual education and you attended a bilingual program as a child (or if you teach bilingual education now), then that is a potential source of bias. It does not mean you should not study bilingual education, but it means you need to be up front in your methodology about your experiences and explain how you will control for these areas of bias.

Step 3: **Select Your Site, Gain Access, and Get to Your Participants**

Site Selection

Another important component of data collection is your site selection for the study. The site must be one where you can gather appropriate data. The site should have participants that fit the criteria for your study. For example, if you are studying successful bilingual programs, your site would need to be somewhere that has a successful bilingual program. Avoid samples that are chosen out of convenience.

Gain Access

You need a site where you can not only collect quality data, but also where you can gain access. Determine who or what are the gatekeepers for your site—the persons you have to go through to get to your actual participants. As mentioned with Tip 5, you must first have permission to gain access to your site. You should be honest and forthright about what you plan to do and what role you will play at the site. You should also explain what you will do with your findings.

Get to Your Participants

In a qualitative study, your participants determine the quality of the data that you obtain. It is important to examine the appropriateness of your participants for the purpose of your study. Are they willing participants (which should always be the case, if the study is ethical)? Are your participants honest and trustworthy—do they stand to lose or gain anything by participating in the study? What level of bias do you have towards the participants, and/or they towards you as the researcher? Can you build a rapport with these participants, in order to obtain valid and reliable data from your interviews? Another issue to consider with your participants is the actual interview process. How long should your interviews be? How many people should you interview? Can you accomplish the number of interviews you want or need in the timeframe that you have for the study? What other kinds of data do you need to support your interview results? Do you have access to the participants you need, and/or to the supplemental data as well? All of these questions must be answered in order for adequate data collection to take place.

Remember that your sample is purposeful—describe the participants in detail (they *are* your study). You chose these persons for a reason, so be sure that your readers know what this reason is and how your participants fit this need.

A Final Comment

Be detailed in your descriptions – We should be able step by step to replicate your study based on the description of your data collection of your methodology. This is vitally important in a qualitative study, where we do not have "statistical significance" or the benefit of mathematical computations to validate our results.

Target Activities

 Target 8.   Collect Your Data

A.   For each of the types of data, list the advantages and disadvantages of each as they pertain to your particular study.

	Advantages	Disadvantages
Interviews		
Observations		
Focus Groups		
Documents		
Survey		

B.   Based on the advantages and disadvantages you identified above, which type(s) of data are most appropriate for achieving your purpose?

_____

_____

_____

_____

C.   List 10 things about yourself that could be potential areas for bias in a qualitative research study.   Then, consider how you would control for each of these, or what techniques you would engage in to minimize the impact of bias.

1. _____

2. _____

3. _____

4. _____

5. _____

6. _____

7. _____

8. _____

9. _____

10. _____

D.   Consider the problem and purpose of your study. Consider your research questions. Now develop interview questions that will help provide data to answer your research questions. List your interview questions below.

1. _____

2. _____

3. _____

4. _____

5. _____

6. _____

7. _____

8. _____

9. _____

Now, practice these questions with a partner. Include all of the interview formalities, including introducing yourself, explaining the purpose and procedures of your study, turning on the tape recorder, and so on.

When you have completed the interview, ask your partner to critique your interview techniques. He/she can tell you what went well, and what still needs work. You should be able to gauge the effectiveness of your questions as well. Were they clear to your participant? Did he/she know what you were asking, or did you have to clarify?

Now look at the responses you received. Did your questions yield the data that you need to address your problem and purpose? If not, you know that you need to modify your questions. Even the most interesting questions and the most exciting responses are no good if they do not address your problem and purpose. Remember, your study is designed to answer your research questions – make sure your interview questions can accomplish this task.

E.   One more exercise for improving the quality of your interviews -- practice interviewing with the less than ideal respondent. Have your partner choose one of the following characteristics:

1. Shy
2. Argumentative
3. Unresponsive (off task)
4. Verbose
5. Intimidating
6. Intimidated

Now practice your interview again, dealing with one of these types of respondents. How can you adjust the interview so as to still obtain usable data?

How can you maintain your own composure in the face of these types of issues?

While it may seem obvious, practicing these situations can help you avoid "wasting" one of your actual interviews when surprises such as these arise. Also, depending on your topic, there might be other potential interview pitfalls to consider (sensitive topics often lead to sensitive interviews).

Be sure that you receive feedback from your partner after the interview about both the structure and style of the interview as well as the content of your questions. Doing so will save you much time and trouble when you go into your first "real" interview.

TIP #9 ANALYZE YOUR DATA

Once you have collected all of your data, transcribed your interviews, and compiled all of your observation notes, you need to analyze these data. In other words, it is time to make meaning of all these findings. The analysis becomes like a sifter—you put in the flour, the salt, the sugar, the nutmeg—then sift—the results are a smooth texture which can be used to bake the cake. The flour and other ingredients are like the components, the data, the basic input of information and observation—then sifted together, you will be able to see the whole in terms of meaningful connections and relationships.

Step 1: Use the Researcher Interview Observation Notes Checklist and Code the Data

With Tip #8 you collected your data. Hopefully you tape recorded your interviews and have now had them transcribed. You should also have taken notes during the interview process. One way of taking notes during an interview is through a checklist of observable behaviors. The **Researcher Interview Observation Notes** checklist is one sample of this technique. Such a checklist, as seen in Figure 9.1, allows you to quantify non-verbal behaviors that occurred during the interview in case these behaviors support your findings and themes. Certain behaviors can support participant feelings of nervousness, frustration, boredom, or reservation, which can then be used to support or refute the interview findings.

The main technique used for analyzing qualitative data, particularly interview transcripts, is *coding*. Coding involves assigning set codes to certain characteristics or recurring themes within your data. For example, every time the notion of "faculty support" occurs in your transcript, you mark it with an FS. It is important that your codes have meaning and make sense to you as the researcher.

Another good technique to help with data analysis is *memoing*. Rather than assigning simple codes to the interview transcript or notes, a researcher can memo on the pages. This means that you write yourself notes in the margins of the paper; these notes could be questions, remarks, or issues that you have with particular passages in the text.

Many qualitative researchers also keep a journal as they collect and analyze data. *Journaling* allows you to record your own thoughts and feelings as you conduct your study. This way you can sort out your own feelings and gauge on a regular basis how you feel about your study and its participants, etc.

Researcher Interview Observation Notes

Interviewer_____   Time: _____

Participant: _____   Location: _____

Date:_____

Observations	Interview Questions											
	1	2	3	4	5	6	7	8	9	10	11	12
Articulate												
At ease												
Changes seating position												
Clenches hands												
Confident												
Crosses legs												
Decisive in answer												
Direct												
Emotional when replying												
Enthusiastic response												
Fidgets												
Folded arms												
Great eye contact												
Hand gestures												
Hesitation before answering												
Honest and sincere												
Looks around the room												
Looks into air while thinking												
Nervous												
Passionate in response												
Pauses to think before answering												
Quick to answer												
Reassuring facial expression												
Relaxed posture												
Relaxed while answering												
Rolls eyes while answering												
Rubs head/eyes												
Searches for words												
Shakes foot												
Smiles after answering												
Wrings hands												
Other:												

General Comments:

Figure 9.1. **Interview checklist**

Target Activities

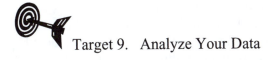
Target 9.   Analyze Your Data

A.   For the interview transcript below, develop a series of codes to analyze your data. Analyze the transcript using these codes, and identify a set of themes that seem to occur in these data. You can also use memoing as you analyze the data, in addition to simple coding.

Codes for these data:

_____   _____   _____

_____   _____   _____

_____   _____   _____

_____   _____   _____

_____   _____   _____

Recurring themes that appear in this passage:

Theme 1: _____

Theme 2: _____

Theme 3: _____

Theme 4: _____

Theme 5: _____

Interview
Parent Number 1
December 5, 2005

Interviewer – Ir
Translator – Tr (Joy)
Parent – P1m (mother)
        P1f (father)

[This first interview took place at the restaurant owned by the parents. The Interviewer and Translator arranged to meet at a time that is usually quiet at the restaurant. Background music competed with the clarity of the recording, and the parent (mother) has a very soft-spoken demeanor. Since this interview was conducted almost entirely in Spanish, a general overview is provided in this first document regarding the interview. As an English speaker not proficient in her understanding of Spanish, the Interviewer is not able to provide a complete verbatim translation from Spanish to English. Brackets
 [ ] indicate words in Spanish not understood or words inaudible on the tape, as well as probable English translations of the segment of the interview. *More sizeable passages that need to be translated later are written in italics*]

Ir: Hello! Thank you so much. And these are so... What a treat. Thank you! (All eating chips and salsa.)

Ir: Well, is it easier for me to speak English or for you to translate?

Tr: Do you want me to translate or for her to speak Spanish?

P1m: (Answer not audible)

Tr: It doesn't matter.

Ir: OK, we'll just try and see. Well, thank you for doing this with us.And, this is for the parents – the relatives – of children in Project Ella, um, it is something that you can read and answer. Either now or later. [The interviewer gave P2 a copy of *Proyecto ELLA Encuestra Para Los Padres*]. The reason for us being here is to talk. This is like…

P1m: Extra.

Ir: Extra, yeah.

Tr: This was given to your child by the teacher. It came through the office.

Ir: [The interviewer noticed that P1m seemed hesitant about completing the *Encuestra* (survey)] But you could have that, and it is … almost the same as this , sort of.

Tr: Almost the same.

P1m: Oh, um hum.

Ir: So, do you want to just start talking about this?

P1m: Yes.

Ir: OK. Um, well let me get to the English so that I can read. Um, first, you know, Cindy Guerrero says that this is a good question: What would you like to know about Project ELLA? (Cindy Guerrero was P1's son's pre-kindergarten teacher the previous year, and there seemed to be mutual affection and positive esteem between former teacher, student, and student's family.)

Tr: If you would like to know about Project ELLA. If you have questions or want to know about the program…

P1m: Well, now it is very good. I like it a lot. Helping the children a lot… [… Maybe saying something like it is not helping with computation?]

Tr: Yesterday, yes. And you don't help on Saturdays?

P1m: Not right now – they can't right now because there are other things so they have less time for that […]

Tr: Now, yes. (laughter)

Ir: Do you have examples? Um, do you have examples of your child's growth in speaking English since this time last year?

Tr: Do you have examples of your child's growth in speaking English since this time last year?

P1m: What kind of examples?

Tr: Examples like have you seen more English spoken at home, or when you go to stores, or…

P1m: Oh, no, he always speaks in English.

Ir: Oh, really?

P1m: Yeah, he has two languages, but he speaks more English. In the normal English class, he speaks two languages perfectly. […]

Tr: Oh, OK.

P1m: Spanish. The young one is bilingual. The teachers were surprised. Two languages at the same time. The words are perfect.

Ir: Is that because of Project ELLA, do you think?

Tr: [repeated the above in Español]

P1m: Well, I say yes.

Tr:

P1m: But I really like Project ELLA.

Ir: OK. I think I got… I think I understand (laughter) Um, can you provide specific examples of your child's growth in reading English since last year.

Tr: Now in reading – Have you seen growth?

P1m: Can you say he reads perfect English and perfect Spanish? Yes, both languages. Other children read at most 50 words, and he reads 99 words.

P1m: Yes, double. _ (P1 said this with a great amount of pride, and a large smile on her face.)

Ir: You mentioned that the other day.

P1m: Yes.

Ir: (Interviewer noticed that P1 was looking at another table that needed service) Do you need to do something else? I know you were looking at the other table. If you need to do something. (P1 asked someone to get the drink order from the table she was watching.)

Tr: [Do you think this is because of your child, or because of Project ELLA?]

Ir: Can you give some examples of times that you were surprised to see Israel using English?

Tr: Examples of times that you were surprised to see him using English – what surprised you, how he used it with the family, or here?

P1m :How he uses the language, or?

Tr: […] Yes, I also speak to him.

P1m: Oh, does that surprise the customers?

Tr: Oh yeah?

Ir: Oh!

P1m: Yes, yes. What do the customers say? What grade is he in? And I tell them "first." Bilingual. My little brother is not in English; I am in English. They say, but you speak perfect English.

Ir: Oh, wow!

Tr: Oh, very good!

P1m: And the questions that they ask him, he answers them. [There are things that the younger child, who is in ELLA... speaks more rapidly in English... Doing better in general in English and helps his older brother]

Tr: Ah.

P1m: Sometimes the oldest helps the younger one to [...]

Tr: Yes?

P1m: He speaks perfect English. And there are things that the first child who is in ELLA knows more, and more quickly.

Ir: So, he helps here, with the customers? How good!

P1m: (Looking very pleased). Yes, yes.

(The student's father came up to our table at that time.)

Ir: Oh, ! Good afternoon!

P1f: Hello!

Plm: The ones from ELLA.

Ir: How are you doing?

Ir: Very well, thank you. My Spanish is...(laughter)

Plm: [...] Guerrero. From Cindy Guerrero [...]

P1f: Oh, your Spanish is very good. It is very good that when you come to Mexico you won't have problems with Spanish, right?

Ir: Oh, well. I try.

P1f: Do you practice with the guys over there? (laughter)

Ir: Oh, well. Even more because my husband loves ice cream. He'll say "how do you say butter pecan"! You know... all the types of ice cream.

P1f: OK

Ir: But it's nice to see you again.

P1f: It's nice to see you too.

Ir: This was just a survey that went out to the parents. (Ir. Bringing P1f up to date in the conversation.)

P1f: Uh, huh.

Ir: The questions are similar to the ones we are asking in the interview today. It's that I want to have the words of the parents. Not just the numbers and facts. I want the color of the language.

P1f: I would like to know...

Tr: Yes.

Ir: Things that he likes and does not like.

Tr: She wants to know if the child is doing well.

P1m: (I think the gist of the conversation was that Israel is working with Frankie; teaching his older brother English. We made some comments that Israel is "el maestro," the teacher. That Frankie needs help from ELLA. P1f – father – leaves to go back to work.)

         [A segment that I really do not understand]

Ir: And are you learning English?

P1m: Yes, yes. (I think that she says that her children say, "Mommy is in pre-k.")

Tr: (Laughs)

P1m: Sometimes I am scared… [think she was saying that sometimes she is frightened without the help of her children translating, but that she works mornings at the restaurant without the benefit of anyone to translate, and that she does pretty well taking the orders from a busy crowd.]

Ir: Yeah. OK, well, Joy, do you want to just say "Can you think of any other abilities or attitudes of your child that Project ELLA may impact?

Tr: […] [Repeats gist of above]

P1:   Excuse me?

Tr: Let me see. Can you think of any other ways that Project ELLA can help your child? In other areas…of school… or?   […]

P1m: In other areas of school?

Tr: Yes.

Ir: Some people speak with confidence or, you know, they can go ask questions at the office and ask for things they need in English.

Tr: I think that's good.

P1m: Yes, […] Yes, he is doing well in everything.   He gets all "A"s on his tests. In all of his subjects he gets stickers and notes that say "excellent."

Tr: And does he like school?

P1m: [Yes, he likes school. When her husband wakes him up in the morning, he jumps out of bed to get ready for school.] [She loves the teachers. And the teachers love the children. The teacher that teaches English now is good] Ms. Guerrero era excelente. [P1m has been and is a volunteer at school. She watched Ms. Guerrero, and likes her a lot. ELLA helps them for…]

Tr: And the books that he has read during the year?

P1m: [Oh yes we read them. I love them. Israel would say "Mommy lets me read the books!" I was surprised because Ortega … advanced. Thanks to ELLA, because it motivates them.]

Tr: Yes, he speaks in English. A lot.

Ir: Um, she has two sons, right? An older and the younger, and the older didn't have ELLA?

Tr: Right, the older one that's in ESL.

Ir: Would there be… in comparing the two… any difference that she could see?

Tr: Yes, she talked about that that the older one…   That she's noticed the difference.

Ir: OK. OK. That's what I thought ya'll were.   Um, I was getting …
clarification. (Laughter)

Tr: Yes, she was asking me about my oldest son.

P1m: Uh huh.

Tr: If there was a difference.

P1m: Oh yes, I see a big difference. […]

Tr: He is in all English, right?

P1m: Yes, all English. [… the things that his teacher is teaching him are the things that the younger child is studying.]

Tr: Oh wow.

P1m: It is very different. His teachers says he is very smart, too.   […I think she was taking enchiladas to her older son's teacher. Her older son's teacher commented how well he is doing in school, and she said to the teacher,] "I think," she said, "that

ELLA has helped a lot. I am grateful for ELLA." A discussion followed that is not related to Project ELLA regarding the older son and his teacher. This was followed by a discussion regarding the family's positive regard for Cindy Guerrero, Israel's pre-k teacher. Something about discrimination in the first grade...an incident regarding her older son's class? They are not changing schools.... Changing back to positive comments regarding Cindy Guerrero. She is very pretty. Her husband is going back to take school in computation... That is what he is lacking. Her son wondered if he is taking classes with Ms. Guerrero. Her son thinks Ms. Guerrero is another mother. Pero ella es muy linda.]

Ir: And she likes your son a lot. With her Heart. She showed me a picture of the class and Israel. So cute.

P1m: Si, como ¿Cuándo, Cinco de Mayo? [More discussion about Cinco de Mayo presentation in class. More compliments about Ms. Guerrero... Israel thinks the teachers this year are pretty too. Israel says that he has beautiful teachers that only get mad when the children are really bad] Pero son muy buenos, las maestras. Le enseñan muy bien.

Tr: Esta con Mrs. Dominuguez, ?verdad?

P1m: Si, con Mrs. Domínguez esta ahorita.

Ir: Do you have,... Oh, I'd better say it in Ingles.... Have any suggestions for Project ELLA, or anything that she would like to see in addition to what they are doing?

Tr: [...] anything to recommend? [...] More for the parents? Or more for the teachers, or the children?

P1m: *I need to come back to this section... [The teachers do a lot. Principally when they were in kinder no hay muchos padres to help the teachers. The ELLA teachers tried to motivate. But many children were behind. I liked to go motivate them, to talk. The teachers do a lot, and she thinks the parents should help. She would get on the bus one day a week with Israel and spend the day at school. She thinks parents should see what is going on. Since they opened the restaurant this past year, "que extrañan de los ninos." Going to school helps her stay connected with her children and their school. I always tell them that even though other parents drop off and pick up their children, I want to see what is going on at school. I want to help the teachers. With two...]*

Tr: *What is the motivation for children to work at home? We don't see many parents..*

P1m: *Need to talk with them by telephone. Maybe tell the busy parents to volunteer at school 2 hours, nothing more. The teachers work with the children. Parents need to work after the teachers. It's very hard. Need to practice. I don't want the teachers to give them everything.*

(P1m needed to attend to something in the restaurant. She left the table. The following discussion is between Tr and Ir in the absence of P1m:)

Ir: That's a lovely mother.

Tr: Um hum. She'd be a good parent advocate to have. Like if we needed somebody on the inside to work with parents. Cause coming from the outside is hard. Like it's easier to get parents to come, if you have a parent telling her.

Ir: Gosh, I like her so much. I don't need to take anymore of her time. I was interested to hear what she had to say in addition to what these questions were. It's interesting to me ... a dissertation I read about parent volunteers. Why parents sort of hesitate. I think it is different for Project ELLA because Spanish is spoken so much in schools, but you can just imagine the things that they found in research about parents not feeling welcomed.

Tr: I've walked into some schools in Aldine where you walk in and the receptionist is not very welcoming. And I'm a district employee. And they intimidate me. And I'm like, "Well I'm here for Project ELLA." And I can't imagine if I were a parent… And if you are illegal? That makes it even… you don't even want to step into the school. They can't even call in. The parents don't realize that. The schools don't call; they can't call Immigration.

Ir: Oh. There ought to be a little workshop on that or something.

Tr: So that we could go… "It doesn't matter what your status…" Now, we can't say that they aren't waiting around the corner, but that is not the schools – not our responsibility [to report Illegal status.]

Ir: I tell you the receptionist, the women who greets people at Keeble is so lovely. I love her.

Tr: Um hum.

(P1m returns to the table.)

Ir: I have the books. Is there anything else that you would like for us to know?

P1m: [Not more than the parents. *Come back to this part.* Maybe that there are 100 children, and 20 parents will show up at a meeting. And her talking about how beautiful it would be if all the parents would motivate their children.]

Tr: [I think she responds to the effect of how it would help the teachers as well.]

P1m: [Teachers need help.]

Tr: [How would you motivate more parents (fathers) to be involved? The director? The teacher? What is the most effective manner?]

P1m: [I think that that I can know the problems that the teachers have with the children. I see … The fathers are working…]

Tr: Thank you very much.

P1m: No, thank you.

Ir: Thank you. I am going to listen and learn everything, but I think that the parents' voices are a very important part of this. And I am going to write a setter to you with my number and maybe Joy's.

P1m: Oh, OK. Thank you.

Ir: We have a small gift for you. It is from ELLA. You can choose one in English and one in Spanish.

[She chose books, and discussed with Joy which books were from last year. She had one or two of the books already. She carefully chose the books. Talks again about the books from Ms. Guerrero.]

Ir: Do you have the big book of activities?

P1m: Yes.

Ir: Do you like the activity book?

P1m: Yes.

Ir: That's good. That's wonderful. Thank you very much for the time.   And for the snacks. Then she offered us something to drink and another basket of chips. (Tape turned off).

What themes appear from the data?

_____

_____

_____

How do these themes interact with one another?

_____

_____

_____

Do any sub-themes appear?

_____

_____

_____

How would you describe your findings?

_____

_____

_____

B. Once you have practiced coding above, analyze the data for your own qualitative study.

Codes for my data:

_____   _____   _____

_____   _____   _____

_____   _____   _____

_____   _____   _____

_____   _____   _____

Recurring themes that appear in my analysis:
Theme 1: _____
Theme 2: _____
Theme 3: _____
Theme 4: _____
Theme 5: _____

C.   Describe your data analysis procedures for your study. This should include exactly what you did to accomplish your findings. Include things such as transcribing the interviews, coding the transcripts, recoding, analyzing codes for recurring themes, and other such methods of data analysis. As with data collection, this description should be clear, detailed, and replicable.

_____

_____

_____

_____

_____

_____

D.   Based on the themes that you found in your data, write your findings of the study. Your findings should describe what you found meaningful in your data. At this point, you are simply describing these findings. You can support your themes with powerful direct quotes from the interview transcripts.

_____

_____

_____

_____

_____

TIP #10 WRITE THE PAPER, REVISE, AND EDIT

If you have successfully maneuvered through Tips 1 through 9, then you should be ready to put your paper together. And we mean exactly that—put it together. The point of working logistically on your component parts in a sequential order is to have a completed product that nicely fits together and is ready to turn in or publish.

Step 1: Know Your Parts

Your final paper should consist of the following parts:

Introduction
Problem
Purpose
Review of Literature
Theoretical Framework
Methodology
       Context
       Sample
       Instrument
       Data Collection
       Reliability and Validity
       Data Analysis
Findings
Conclusions and Implications

You may or may not use these titles as your headings and subheadings, but the information suggested by these titles should be easily identified. As you put these parts together, make sure that you include transitions that help the paper read smoothly as you move from one part to the next.

You should also have large amounts of raw data—notes, interview transcripts, coding sheets, documents, etc.—that support all of your findings. You do not need to include these pages in your actual paper, but you should keep them organized in a safe place so that your paper and its findings can be verified at any time. You should also keep your IRB approval with these documents.

Step 2: Write Your Conclusions and Implications

By now you should have all of the above components completed except for your conclusions and implications. This part of your paper should be the most enjoyable to write—it is your opportunity to express yourself and to put your own "flavor" into the study.

The conclusions are those ideas that are based on your actual findings. If, for example, you find that *teacher satisfaction* was the most commonly occurring theme in your study of successful bilingual programs, then you could draw conclusions regarding the impact of successful programs on teachers' satisfaction with their jobs. Keep in mind that qualitative research can never be used to determine causality, but it can be used to determine clarify relationships and develop understanding. Thus, you as the researcher can draw conclusions based on your data.

Implications are a description of what impact your findings and conclusions could have on others, whether this impact be on teachers, students, administrators, school districts, parents, university programs, or other researchers. Implications can be far-reaching and may be offered for practice or for further research. Implications can also lead to recommendations in these areas (practice and research) as well.

One common problem with novice researchers is that they sell themselves short on conclusions and implications. They will spend 15-20 pages describing their related literature and methods, and then offer a page or less of conclusions and implications. This is your chance to shine, to show the rest of us why your study was important. It is the "so what" of your study—the part where you get to impress upon readers what was valuable in your study and how that value impacts other stakeholders. Take advantage of this opportunity. You put a great deal of effort into ensuring that your study was conducted using a sound research base and sound methodology. Now demonstrate that it paid off, that your findings are important for the rest of us. Give us the "so what."

Target Activities

Target 10.   Write the Paper, Revise, and Edit

A. Write the Conclusions and Implications sections for your paper.

B. Edit. One of the critical, and often overlooked, components to your final paper is editing. Combs (2005) developed an Editing Checklist suitable for use with a qualitative paper. This list will help you ensure that your paper is in top quality shape from a technical standpoint, which is a must if you plan to turn this paper in for a grade or publish it as a piece of scholarly work.

A few checkpoints to go through as you finalize your paper:
- Go through the paper and be sure that you have followed all rules for APA style; there is no excuse for errors of this type in your final draft.
- Cross check your reference section with the references in the text. Everything cited in the paper must be in the reference section, and everything in the reference section should likewise be cited in the paper. Be sure all of these match up as well in terms of the spelling of authors' names, dates of publication, and other critical information.
- Be sure that your paper is written in past tense. The study is now completed, so there is absolutely no future tense allowed.
- Remember that the intent of this paper is a scholarly article—that is how it should read. It is not a dissertation, but neither is it informal.
- Have a peer edit your final draft—it really helps.

Editing Checklist for Final Draft

Overall Mechanics

_____ Did you proofread and edit your paper carefully?

_____ Did you perform a final spell-check and grammar-check of each section?

_____ Are your margins set appropriately?

_____ Is your paper double-spaced? (See tables for special formatting)

_____ Is the font consistent and 12 point?

_____ Is every paragraph indented 5-7 spaces?

_____ Did you space one time after punctuation marks at the end of a sentence? After commas, colons, and semicolons? After periods in citations? After periods of the initials in personal names?

_____ Did you use a comma between elements, including _and_ and _or_ in series of 3 or more items?

_____ Did you use bulleted lists? Bulleted lists are not permitted in APA; items are set apart in paragraphs with letters or numbers (a), (b), and (c)…or in a numbered list (see APA p. 292)

_____ Did you check for consistency in the entire document concerning the use of hyphenated words (e.g. burnout at-risk)? Use the dictionary when in doubt.

_____ Bold type is not permitted for any headings or words in APA (See heading formats, APA pp. 289-290.)

Style and Language Usage

_____ If you used Latin abbreviations (i.e., e.g., etc.), are they in parentheses, and have you checked for the required punctuation?

_____ If you have used long quotations are they absolutely necessary? Include page numbers from original sources for all direct quotes. See APA for blocking 40+ words and for format of quotes (p. 118).

_____ Does each direct quotation contribute significantly to the review?

_____ Can any of these quotations be paraphrased?

_____ Have you avoided slang terms and colloquialisms?

_____ Have you avoided using contractions?

_____ Have you spelled out all acronyms on first mention?

_____ If you have used first person, was it appropriate?

_____ Have you avoided using sexist language?

_____ If you used numbers in the narrative of your review, have you checked to see is you spelled out the numbers zero through nine? (APA p. 122)

_____ If you used a noun followed by a number to denote a specific place in a sequence, did you capitalize the noun?

_____ If you used a number to begin a sentence, did you spell it out? (APA p. 122)

Grammatical Accuracy

_____ Is every sentence of your paper a complete sentence?

_____ Have you avoided using indirect sentence constructions (as in, "In Galvan's study, it was found…")?

_____ Have you been consistent in your use of tenses (e.g., past tense in describing study's findings)?

_____ If you have any long sentences, have you tried to break them down into two or more sentences?

_____ If you have any long paragraphs, have you tried to break them down into two or more paragraphs?

Accuracy of Citations and References

_____ Have you checked APA for citing references in the narrative (e.g., when to use parentheses, how to cite multiple authors, and how to cite a secondary source)?

_____ Have you checked each citation in the text to make sure that it appears on your reference list?

_____ Have you checked all entries on the reference list to make sure that each one is cited in your text?

_____ Have you eliminated all entries from your reference list that are not cited in the text?

_____ Have you checked for accuracy and consistency between the spelling of the dates in your text and the dates in your reference list?

_____ Have you checked for the accuracy and consistency between the spelling of the authors' names in your text and in your reference list?

_____ Are most of the dates of the studies included in the reference list within the recent past?

Other things to check for…

_____ Are all required parts included and described in sufficient detail? (methodology, data analysis, findings, reliability and validity, etc.)

_____ Is there consistent use of subject/verb & subject/pronoun agreement?

_____ Is it readable?

_____ Is it coherent? Are there appropriate transitions?

_____ Is the title page correct?

_____ Is there a running head?

_____ Is there an abstract?

_____ Are headings used correctly?

Name of author_____

Name of proofreader_____

Date_____

Source: Combs, J. (2005). Editing checklist. Unpublished work. Sam Houston State University, Hunstville, TX.

C.   Use the Irby Qualitative Critique to critique a qualitative study you found in your review of literature that you liked; then critique your completed study. This Critique provides a way for you to self impose quality control and also a way to revise and edit your paper.

One more way to edit your final paper and be sure that it is of top quality is to critique your own work. Not just editing, which looks at mechanics, grammar, and other technical aspects of your writing. We mean *critique,* evaluate your paper on its overall merits and ensure that everything that should be in the paper is actually there. The following Qualitative Research Critique (Irby, 2006) offers a good way to critique your paper. Remember, it behooves you to be as critical and exact with your own work as possible, since it soon will be turned in for review by your professor or for critical review for publication.

Irby Qualitative Research Critique

Summarize the study with the following side headings.

1. Bibliographic Information (APA Style)

2. Problem: What is the problem or need? Is it stated clearly? Logical? Convincing?

3. Purpose: What is the use or purpose? Does it focus the research? Does the purpose follow the problem statement logically? Are you convinced from the researcher this study is worthwhile?

4. Theoretical Framework: Is there evidence of grounded theory for the research? Is it well-established?

5. Prior research or Literature review: What previous work has been done leading up to this study? Is there any major body of research missing?

6. Method research question(s): What is/are the research question(s)? Are the research questions specific and clear? Are the research question(s) related to the purpose?

7. Method--Data Collection and Analysis: Are participants, sampling techniques, and context for the study explicit and appropriate? Is the research design clear? Are the collection and analysis based on solid referenced methods? Are the methods the best choice in the study? What improvements would you suggest?

8. Definition(s): Which terms are defined? Are the definitions operational? Are the definitions included within the introduction or within the methods section of the report?

9. Credibility and reliability issues in design: What does the author say regarding issues of credibility and/or generalizing ability internal and/or external validity? Respond to each of the internal/external validity issues. Check each one to see if the item is included or if the item has been overlooked.

---

10. Method instrumentation: Describe the instrument(s) for interviews, focus groups, etc. Were they pre-existing, or specially created? How were they related? Ho~ was reliability established?

11. Ethics: Does the author discuss ethical issues? Do you see any ethical issues in the study? Are the ethical issues properly taken care of?

12. Limitations and delimitations: What limitations/delimitations are identified? How do these limit generalizability? To what extent do the limitations/delimitations (stated or unstated) affect the value of the research?

13. Results and Discussion: Are the research questions answered? Is existing literature brought into the discussion? Are supportive/representative statements used from the data when appropriate?

14. Implications and recommendations: What are the implications/recommendations for theory, further research, and/or practice?

Source: Irby, B.J. (2006). Qualitative research critique. Unpublished work. Sam Houston State University, Huntsville, TX.

D.   Timeline for Completing this Project in One Semester

If you want to complete a qualitative study in one semester, then you will have to have a very focused, disciplined timeline. Based on a traditional 15-16 week semester, we offer the following suggested timeline for producing a worthwhile qualitative study in a single semester. While some studies may need more time for certain sections, particularly data collection and analysis, this timeline is a general guideline for what steps will be required to complete such a project. Schedule your project.

Week 1 – topic

Week 2 – problem

Week 3 – purpose

Week 4 – IRB

Week 5 – develop literature review

Week 6 – establish theoretical framework

Week 7 – write methodology

Week 8 – collect data

Week 9 – collect data

Week 10 – write reliability and validity

Week 11 – analyze data

Week 12 – analyze data

Week 13 – write paper

Week 14 – final editing

Week 15 – completed paper, submit for publication

In Conclusion…

You have now put together a qualitative study and critiqued your own results. What have you learned? What can you do better next time? What can you improve within this study? Reflect on the process you used for developing this study: what would you change? What are your thoughts about qualitative studies?

_____

_____

_____

_____

_____

_____

_____

References

Combs, J. (2005). Editing checklist. Unpublished work. Sam Houston State University, Hunstville, TX.

Irby, B.J. (2006). Qualitative research critique. Unpublished work. Sam Houston State University, Huntsville, TX.